Emotions in
Evolution

I0585487

The Poetic Journey Continues

Barbara
Strickland

Copyright © 2017 Barbara Strickland Updated 2018
www.brstrickland.com
Barbara Strickland asserts the moral right to be identified as the author of
this work. All rights reserved

No part of this book may be reproduced or transmitted in any form or by
any means, electronic or mechanical, including photocopying, recording or
any information storage and retrieval system, without prior permission in
writing from the author, nor be otherwise circulated in any form of binding
or cover other than that in which it is published and without a similar
condition including this condition being imposed on the subsequent
purchaser.

The names, characters and events portrayed in this publication other than
those clearly in the public domain, are fictitious and the work of the
author's imagination. Any resemblance to real persons, living or dead is
purely coincidental.

ASIN B07HVYQ94V
ISBN 9780648071532
ISBN 9780648071556

Extracts

Emotions in Eruption Copyright © 2018 Barbara Strickland (2017)
Unexpected Obsession Copyright © 2017 Barbara Strickland (2016)
Unexpected Passion Copyright © 2018 Barbara Strickland
The Narrow Hallway Copyright © 2018 Barbara Strickland

Author's note: This book was written in Australia and uses
British/Australian spelling conventions such as 'colour' instead of 'color',
and 'ise' endings instead of 'ize' on words like 'realize'. Some words will
also have double ll in its spelling e.g. travel will become travelling.

Images by Kathy Johnson
kathymareejohnson@gmail.com

Cover design and illustration by Christopher Brunton
http://www.cjbrunton.wix.com/brunton-illustration

DEDICATION

To Rose and Vince (my parents),

I wish I had your poems to translate Rose, but reading your writing was an impossible feat. Your scribbling, Vince, was constant, and so is mine. My love for education came from you. Share this with me, it's the best I can do without you here, let you share what you helped create.

To my dearest friend Gail.

I carry the memory of your courage. You are now with someone who will love you and keep you, safe forever. I will miss you always. (Don't worry, we will make it to Norfolk Island, just give me a little more time and keep your fingers crossed)

Acknowledgements

Sean and Kathy, thank you for your help on this project. You have both been incredible. Whatever I have asked, you have done. Your time will come. I know it.

Pat, I couldn't have done this without your help. Julia and Sue, Rosie and Vanessa, you guys are great for listening to me rave, and still supporting me. Thank you to all my family members for not doubting my ability to do this even when I did, and lastly thank you to RS for never letting me give up. You are the wise owl on my shoulder and the butterfly wings that keep me afloat.

Table of Contents

Welcome
to
Emotions

Foreword

Emotions in Evolution

I have surprised myself by wanting to do another poetry book. Then again, maybe I am not so surprised. The freedom poetry allows is addictive, liberating and an adrenalin donation I was not expecting. For me poetry is a welcome donor to my ever growing, need for energy.

The world is ravenous for our energy. Being busy is the normal these days, but tired people lose creativity. Evolution can only come and thrive from fresh and creative approaches in all aspects of our lives. We need to nurture whatever feeds our energy. For me the addition of poetry has been quite a revelation. When I finish a piece I feel energised, like a weight has lifted I didn't know I carried.

I have looked at the world as a series of landscapes as you will see. The topics within this are random. The commonality is always the evolution of emotions. Emotions are our connection to each other and I like that connection. In my first poetry book my emotions erupted, in this they are on the road to evolving.

Attempting to put my small stamp on an art form that humbles me is challenging and satisfying. Putting words together in a disciplined form clarifies perspective, overhauls your mind-set. Mine certainly needed that to happen. I can't help wondering if others out there feel the same. Selfishly I find that an exciting and invigorating idea.

If you have read Emotions in Eruption you will know I have a love for the Haiku. I was and still am a novice but the determination to master it grows daily. I love the stunning simplicity of the form and it has led me to embrace the Cinquain. This too thrives on simplicity but allows a little more room for expression. Both forms clamour for the right choice of words. I confess I am addicted to the structure of both these forms. The following is a little bit of information you might find interesting. My research is still in the early stages and in any case, I was more interested in the essence of these two forms.

The Haiku, Japanese in origin, is based on a pattern of syllables. Traditionally it is broken into three lines of five syllables, seven syllables, and five syllables on the last line, however stress is different for the Japanese language. It makes sense that we needed to re-think things. These days the form is not so strict. Often a haiku can be one or two lines in length. The important thing is to be concrete and concise. A haiku will capture a single moment in just a few words and do it with rich imagery. The goal with a haiku is the creation of an image in the mind of the reader, one celebrating beauty and nature with sensitivity.

The challenge to achieve this, whilst difficult, is also something that plucks the best from the poet's imagination. It draws the aspiring poet into a world where expressing emotions in a condensed fashion becomes an all-consuming fever. The haiku makes any topic a source of inspiration and cuts through human experience and cultural boundaries. I love bonsai for the same reason. You can express so much through the smaller, more delicate form, you can encapsulate emotion. I have tried to walk both the traditional path, and one in which I have experimented. Please, bear in mind I am a novice and comments are most welcome.

The cinquain, on the other hand, is an example of shape poetry, and one demanding a more exact number of words for each line of the five lines required. This rigidity creates a unique, symmetrical shape with interesting and descriptive words. However, with the passing of time variable have arisen and these often appear contradictory. I decided I would take the essence and adopt the style often used in schools to get student creative juices flowing.

The first word is a noun and forms the title. The second line consists of two adjectives and the third consists of three 'ing' participles. The fourth line is a phrase and then the last line another noun. This must be a synonym for the title word. The restrictions are like a puzzle. Instead of pieces we position words in a manner that allows them to be autonomous narrators.

Along with these two poetry forms came a fascination for colour in nature. The different shades and depths spoke of stories and I wondered if I could use colour as a muse, and if colour itself was enough. Linking it to life began to make sense. Colours are everywhere in nature. Do individual colours have a meaning? I found that they have, they have a surprisingly extensive vocabulary of their own, as do plants. They have a vocabulary and an incredible history. Plants have long been used medicinally and often nefariously in in magic.

And then I had another thought, what about flowers? They are conspicuously present on birthdays, funerals, graduation and weddings, thus forming an integral part of our lives. Most people know a red rose stands for romantic love and that one does not send yellow roses to anyone in mourning. Most people don't consider flower meanings but when I checked I found some amazing results. Like plants, they have their own aligned meanings, creating a language all their own.

Bombarded with possibilities, I found myself caught in a sudden thunderstorm without an umbrella. Drops of rain beat down hitting my skin, each drop screaming with an idea of its very own, including a link to my novels. Travel is a big part of my books and I wondered whether I could narrow down the individuality of different countries into the smoothness of seventeen syllables. It turned out to be fun trying.

Have I done a good job manipulating words and emotions? You decide, and feel free to let me know what you think. I would be most delighted to make changes, improvements and take new ideas on board. Already I have new ideas for new forms of poetry to explore, so stop me while you can.

Welcome to Emotions in Evolution

Barbara Strickland

2018

Landscapes
(The World in Verse)

The world in which we live dictates our behaviour and influences the way we think. The world however is complex and made up of divisions, both subtle and obvious, conflicting and confusing and blurring the lines where limits might exist. Those divisions come with impressive resumes, demanding we pay attention, for they too are story tellers and they hold our past and lead us to our future.

We have the physical world, the one that exists around us, man-made, and different to the natural one showcasing landforms, oceans, flora and fauna. And then, there is the world of dreams, our hopes and desires, soul felt and creating an emotional rollercoaster. Lastly there is the controversial supernatural where believers of magic connect. This one we call the psychic realm and its mystical fingers keep us fascinated.

We live and love within these boundaries; they shape us and define us. For me personally they create inspiration to form the collection of words you find on these pages. My thoughts are random and roam each landscape with eyes that feed a brain in evolution.

Distanced

I lay dying.

No-one

 to see.

I lay despairing.

No-one

to listen.

I lay disassociated.

No-one

to care.

When did the lane disintegrate?

When did the path diverge?

When did the road dissipate?

When did the highway dissolve?

When did the freeway disappear?

Talking is not the enemy.

It is the way of the traveller.

No one gave notice

Breathing has become impossible.

The automatic flow now my dead

dearest friend.

Hidden and obstructed

fuelling fires flame

growing, grieving, grasping

holding hard hopelessly

to life lost, unwanted.

Thinking has become anguished.

The unstoppable flow now my live

worst enemy.

Obvious, in full view

the fleeting feelings freeze

groaning grievously grim

heaving hurling horror

for life gone, unrealised.

Where was the warning bell?

Did the landlord forget to give notice?

The F Word

Fear, fright, frigid

fickle, failure, frozen

freedom, flying, feeling

fractious, frenzied, flippant

fashionable, fantastic, fabulous

fleeing, fighting, and falling.

Fragrantly fresh friendships and

freakishly fierce foes.

Words are wispy wisdom.

Words are withered wickedness.

Words are simple silent speakers.

Words are slithering in superficial sounds.

They just flow.

They just exist.

They don't always rhyme

but they can be

manipulating, manoeuvring, mangling

masked mutilators.

They can be

magical, magnificent, meanings

moving mountains.

Why the fuck then, do we choose

a vicious verbal twist so that

semantics become syntax-shaped

weapons creating the

fucking fearful clothed figures

of language failure?

Humane humility, or

'h' words are

so much

nicer.

Swimming in deep water

I float;

my face uplifted.

I drown;

the water shifted.

The pull was strong

and called my name.

I recognised a siren song

from whence it came

but I was not

confident.

I failed to fight.

I am not yet

solvent

and am blinded by light.

I am a weak human creation.

I truly do my best

to ignore the clawing sensation

as I fail each test.

To survive you must make the dive.

That's right, isn't it?

The day to thrive will arrive.

That's true, isn't it?

Knock-knock

I hear the words inside my head.

My sleep broken,

I resist

the incessant pull

until

the tugging pains me,

the force annoys me.

Knock, knock.

Nobody home

but

I hate lies,

I hate self-deceit,

I hate the constant buzz,

and

I give in.

I give up.

I write it down.

I write them down.

Knock, knock.

Words are calling.

Senses and Artistry

A heady seductive combination

of words and senses.

An intoxicating mixture

thoughtfully chosen so

the intricate infused joining is

a harmonious fixture.

Smell reaches out, reaches in

and fills our hearts

with a fragrant pull to please

or to assail like painful sin.

The eager eyes await their turn

to feature in the artistry of

unfolding senses with dazzling colours

to have us learn.

Unconfined the sense of feel,

Of touch, distinguishes between

satin and silk and mineral earth

recognising what is real.

The ears, two tiny shells,

hide from shrieking voices or

bask joyously in music and

clearly defined distant bells.

The tongue, a human elemental,

reaches out to sweet and sour

tantalising and maximising chilli heat

with the blend of spicy oriental.

Sensory artistry whispers

to the waiting words

and asks for the wisdom

to create unique places

and fairy tale moments within

our very own earthly kingdom.

Natural Inspiration

Around me,

surrounds me.

For there is magic

filling my pores,

taking over my senses

on the green hued floors

of sprouting leaves and roots,

inside stick-like branches

and in natural lawns

of fresh smelling and smiling fields.

I seek their calm.

I am avarice for the peace

of different shades that

blend beckoningly, battling

the never ceasing contrasting

seams of bounty the humans only lease.

I seek possession.

I am anxious for title deeds,

for proving ownership

and having rights, and

to reach ruin without replenishing.

Quiet! I hear voices, a question!

Did someone call Earth a rental?

Dream Worlds

There are so many.

Where do we start?

If we choose wrong,

we'll break a heart.

There's the one we want,

the one we crave,

but don't go there

or are you brave?

I'm not. It frightens me.

It lures with promises

and disguises the pitfalls

with romantic premises.

There's the one we call a fantasy.

It's the one where we dare

to dream of the things

we're afraid to share.

Only the hopeful will admit

their thoughts are continuous

and fixated on it.

There's the world where we live.

It's real, it's every day.

It's where I stay.

Those other worlds are not for me.

My mind is locked away without a key.

Hush

Silence, the constant glow of

media light of unending power

in the recesses that never fill,

in the tunnels that lead nowhere, everywhere.

Where did the symphonic sounds of

melodic, maniacal madness go?

Is there a simultaneous event in action?

Is there a juxtaposition

hammering in my head?

There exists a silence of absence.

It is most kind, most respectful.

There is a silence of unheard words.

It is most cruel and most merciless.

On backward glances

Dangerous aging memories

of

an amazing time that bleakly flew,

call you.

Wishing is an unsafe toy

and

regret – a stupid, useless ploy.

Content in a world that moved along

you foolishly turned,

caught up in reckless recollections.

In emotional tethers tangling tenaciously

you glanced in that gilded gold glass

where

you no longer belonged

and

saw torn and tattered lace

and a wrinkled saddened

colour-lacking face.

Time is cruel, brutalising

and

the feathered softness

of

the quilted past

shows bleak, bottomless baffled

eyes

unfocused, downcast

and

the consequence

of

all those lies.

On loving our children

A natural task

but the little horrors wear a mask.

Angelic when they sleep –

by day they write on walls

and make you weep.

They cuddle close and hold on tight

then deny it when they bite.

They fail to see crumbs bring ants galore

and deny spilled drinks bring you more.

Cruel and sweet, kiss or beat,

their challenge a feat and hard to meet

and yet, for them our hearts do beat.

Reassuring sounds

I heard the clock tick.

How strange when

silence of technology

rules.

I heard my heart beat.

And, I pondered for

loneliness of being

reigns.

I heard the dripping of blood.

And, I shut my eyes

against the fear power

commands.

I heard the forced expulsion of breath

and I chose to whimper

ceding all my hard won

control.

I heard the change to nothing.

And I answered with nothing for

stillness had come home to

reside.

My body belongs to the puppeteer.

 My mind knows only to follow.

Un-coordinated, unable to resist

the final fear I swallow.

Thank you for turning off the machine.

Psychic communication

The connections take me prisoner.

I can't avoid the sun, the moon

and the sky above, and

the air I breathe.

The land holds me,

grounds me and gives me life.

I am a part of it,

a part of the greater,

a part of the more

I don't understand.

They, it, all that it is

holds me

with its power.

For the world is magical

and if I honour its apparitions

then power will yield

to me and I will

commune with the universe

and not just the world

around me.

Don't forget to analyse

Soundless whispers are welcome.

Alone in our mind

the truth gets caught

forcing out

the troubled thought,

twisting it, turning it

into things best left unsaid

leaving our soul unfed.

Don't look so hard!

Don't turn around!

Certainly, most of all

don't make a sound.

Ignore what you can.

Accept what is possible

for you,

a mortal man.

For we are told

that to question

interprets too often

as far too bold.

What then?

Oblivion?

It is good to comprehend.

Wise to hesitate before pressing send.

Despite what appears an obvious link

there is a necessity

telling us to stop and think.

Analysing improves capacity

our brains expand and forgo the Shrink.

I am a shadow

Faded, worn and lost

because the process makers

ignore the aging cost.

I am a wraith

almost transparent now.

My colours blur and dilute

and my spirit despairs

at the naivety of the so called astute.

I am a whisper of wind

to voices, lingeringly loud

demanding the attention,

the rights of the belligerent proud.

And suddenly it matters not

that they forgot.

For I have dissipated,

have been obliterated

and now to my surprise

finally

I am liberated.

Love, it takes all kinds

The Greeks had seven words for love and I thought I might explore this in prose. My leading lady Alexia in Unexpected Passion is Greek, and I think she is exerting a greater influence than I first suspected. I hope so as she is quite the character.

The bane of our existence.

The reason for our evolution.

The reason for human persistence.

The emotion that lacks solution.

The *Ancient Greeks* gave us insight.

Separated views of love, have might.

Eros was erotic and sexual.

Agape selfless and sacrificial.

Ludus played, flirted, seduced.

Philia to friendship, platonic was reduced.

Pragma we all hope to obtain

for *Pragma* is shared love and

the one we all hope to retain.

Why not, when it means

long-standing, a couple's refrain.

And now we move to self-love

or *Philautia* by name.

A puzzle, often a nuisance from above

when narcissism is the game.

But then self-love can be enabling

giving us a noble redemption

when we lose the ego labelling

with caring as our intention.

And when *Storge* deems to reveal

we find the best is last

for familial has nothing to conceal

as parent and child, love holds fast.

What now, we ask?

Do divisions ease the task?

But love remains the eternal mystery

controlling lives all through our history.

Losing Love

Drifting slow and hitting fast

from the awful spell you cast

I move away and hope to keep

the sorrow from burrowing

into my soul so deep.

You didn't listen as I spoke,

refused what I chose to evoke.

I sat quietly and replied

and hid the telling sounds I sighed.

How many times now has agony fed

upon the failure of what I said?

The Heart and the Alphabet

Wings whispering,

earnest exchanging,

harsh hammering,

angry advancing,

deadly dancing,

useless urging

outside my skin,

and inside my head.

My beating heart,

is confused but keeps up.

Clouds circling,

softly singing,

ornate offering,

gently gifting,

peaceful pondering,

quiet questioning,

inside my skin,

and outside my head.

My beating heart needs

to settle down.

Talons tingling,

madly menacing,

vicious venting,

ragged reasoning,

keenly kicking,

laborious listening,

outside my skin,

and inside my head.

My beating heart is confused again

and speeds up.

Feathers fluttering,

innocent idling,

bashful believing,

noiseless nodding,

youthful yielding,

judicious juggling,

inside my skin,

and outside my head.

My beating heart splutters,

slowing down.

The scales are weighted,

balanced, and fair.

The heart is not sold,

won't credit images as fated,

won't listen, doesn't dare,

wants it to end, to fold.

Inside, outside the skin.

Inside, outside the head.

The puzzle pieces are thin.

Zing. The heart stops.

Zap. The heart is dead.

Outside my window

Little bird, little bird,

go find somewhere else to play.

I hate your cheeping voice.

Find somewhere far away

because quiet is my choice.

I want to dream, to sleep,

not listen to the high-pitched call.

Yet I hear it, I hear it creep,

wanting, daring to enthral.

It has awakened my heart

with its trill and flapping wings.

It has pierced the deepest part.

It has that power when it sings.

Does the winged one call

because I am feeling sad?

Does it deliberately enthral

because it wants me glad?

No light fills my heart

despite the power of those wings.

Sharp ear piercing on its part

despite the pretty way it sings.

It knows I need to take the leap

and refuses to let me ignore his call.

It knows my unhappiness is deep

and knows I need it to enthral.

Little bird, little bird, don't leave,

don't go away. I was wrong.

I can't start my day without

your sweet, sweet song.

The Revolution

Listen. Listen to the rain.

Listen as it falls.

Pay attention to the wind.

Listen as it calls.

Listen. Listen to each other.

Break down those walls.

Pay close attention to the truth.

before it palls.

Evolution or a revolution?

Listen. Listen to the land.

Listen as it rumbles.

Pay attention to the sea.

Listen as it tumbles.

Listen. Listen to the earth.

Watch as the human fumbles.

Pay close attention to our earth

before it crumbles.

Reconstruction or deconstruction?

If we listen to the revolution

we may just reach our evolution.

If we don't think about deconstruction

we may never get to reconstruction.

Resonating Changes

Polar bears are drowning.

I heard that somewhere.

Suddenly I was frowning

And awake enough to care.

What action will it take

for it to truly resonate?

What disruption must we make

for us to truly question fate?

For everything else we do,

we stop to make a plan or two.

Seems strange to hesitate.

Seems odd to refuse the date

when all the earth begs to ask

is a portion of our love

choosing, a small but valid task,

to keep the sky above,

CLEAN.

When all the earth begs to ask,

is a portion of our busy day

choosing, a small but valid task

to preserve our oceans where we play,

CLEAN.

It begins in our home.

It starts with us, alone.

It spreads in rapid haste.

Preventing thoughtless waste.

Find your polar bear.

Find your way to care.

Home sweet home

Buildings made of steel,

stone, plaster, cement, low-rise

or high-rise. Wait a minute,

aren't those blue jeans?

Bricks, mortar, timber

and re-enforced glass,

all materials, creating,

establishing, an abode

from which to look at

the world, and consider

the world and maybe,

one to keep us safe.

Hay, mud, animal skins,

leaves, tree trunks, sand,

caves, holes underground, and

tunnels, boats large and small.

Well, the places exist.

What makes an abode,

a habitat – a home?

Well, it appears we forgot the

people. Was that deliberate?

Heaven becomes hell.

And the oasis drifts back to desert.

A love letter to the girl that was

It starts as a rose bud.

Tiny tender petals

of youth, of not knowing,

until the bud explodes.

And the sweet, untouched flesh

bleeds with longing as it settles.

There were thorns that lingered,

thorns that pricked,

the unsuspecting digits.

Thorns, not only daring to grasp,

but arrogantly and greedily, fingered.

We took without asking,

assuming our fingerprints had rights

to the leaves of forever young, and

we tainted, misappropriated

while sunshine basking.

Gravity gone

Sometimes I feel the planet

Spinning, turning without me.

Months go by and I

don't understand where the

days, nights have gone.

I don't know where I am

not to feel the pull of gravity,

not to feel my soul cemented to

my body's casing.

Am I in space?

Have I gone, to another world,

another dimension?

No, I am here.

I am alone.

This is what brittles the bone,

despite the hand-held phone

supposedly holding all the voices

with visiting choices.

What a sad refrain

when friends forget

to say your name.

What a cruel, god damned shame.

All I ever wanted

It should have been easy.

It should have flowed.

I'll bet that's what they all said

until the rules were read.

We weren't told it had been decided.

They couldn't chance the questions.

They couldn't allow the impression

that could lead to apprehension.

They prohibited the word, anarchy.

Instead they invented the term, solitary.

That's where I currently reside

and where most days I choose to hide.

All I ever wanted was a peaceful life

but instead I found a well-sharpened knife.

Maybe that's how it's meant to be

and all I ever wanted is right here in front of me.

 A choice would have been nice.

Making the bed

Wake up. Time for life.

Stay asleep. It's far less strife.

I have things I have to do.

Really? Are you sure that's true?

I move. I leave the warmth.

I move again. I leave safety.

I move once more. I hesitate and shake.

Does what I do matter?

I'm already in pieces.

What more can I shatter?

Everything I own has creases.

I turn and make the bed.

I'm alive. Today I thrive.

It's better than the alternate dead.

Quiet, I tell my mind.

Please try to be a little kind.

Please just this once, stop the constant natter.

I sigh as the freshly-made bed diminishes the pitter patter.

Tales of the Unexpected

A Haiku reflection on the great fortune I have experienced travelling to wonderful places. My characters in The Unexpected Series (a contemporary, and a little erotic, romance series) will be fortunate enough to do the same.

Haiku and Travel

Tuscan beauty

enfolds our vision and captures hearts

medieval charm

a fragrant sweep of wine implodes

Venetian glass

glistening gondola glide

bridges sigh

eons of enchanted southern warmth

Mediterranean Sea

Roman Hills cry and whisper timeless tears

of history

dark Gothic remains

Renaissance and Byzantine flavours

travellers return to the golden isle

Sicilian sun

amphitheatre

Olympian laurel green

challenge accepted

ancient hierarchy of ruins

columns standing straight and bold

Turkish taste delight

colourful spice markets smell sweet

Byzantine tiles

arrogant storytelling in mosaic patterns

Rheine castles

magical dark green woods

rippling river flow

clean deep inhale

snow kissed Swiss alpine glory

Vienna woods

atmospheric music in listening leaves

Spanish fiesta

furious flashing Flamenco feet

Portuguese red wine splendour

the Pyrenees call to taste

bonjour sweet pastry

embracing city lovers Parisian style

Nordic gods' splendour

cascade of pure ice

fresh cleansed breath

tulip blanket bold

classic wooden shoes ride proud bicycle paths

London calling card

Big Ben and Convent Garden with fish and chips

Stonehenge majesty

thousands of years held ransom by green fields

Scottish lairds rule

purple rolling hills

Loch Ness myths

Jerusalem hails unique

city of white perched placid and pure

dates in the desert

parched mouths and dry lips breathe in the oasis

salt encrusted sea

memories float inside skins of the avaricious

exotic energy

Casablanca dream

cold marbled magic

pyramid dunes

buried parts and golden desert merge into an oasis

cherry pink scented

blush and bloom

Japanese treasure

Singapore sights

night zoo and orchid garden

monsoon deluge

Harbour Bridge

Opera House and Blue Mountains

sing a Sydney song

Great Barrier Reef

coral views in glass-bottomed boats

turtles

coast of soft silken sand

surfers ride the weaving waves

Australian gold

rainy days

tram travel and city grid

Melbourne glamour

The Colour Connection

Red, yellow, and blue are known as primary colours. Mixed together they create secondary colours. Combining results within those combinations create tertiary colours. It is a complex process that brings a diversity to brighten our lives.

I have always had a soft spot for the Romantic Poets and their love for Nature. Already fascinated by colours and the way they bring life to our world, I wondered if I could put words to the blending and combining, the perfecting of each hue and the embedding of meaning to warm and comfort us.

I wanted to give a voice to the colour connection through the haiku (traditional and more modern), the cinquain and some free verse.

The Primary – The Parents

Blue

Half the world we see

is sky, is ocean.

You hold the key,

the magic potion

of flow, of open spaces

and the freshness of cool

gliding on our faces.

Your colour is an endless pool

where man can dive

and revive.

Blue shades twist and creep

ruling hard with water might.

Liquid leaves the fathoms deep

and sea and sky begin their fight,

ensuring that our planet grows

and the cycle of life evolves,

continuing its highs and lows

as each drop of rain dissolves.

Encouragement for man to strive

and to survive.

Red

Some would argue the powers of hell

hold the reins, ring the bell.

Red is the unquenchable fire

and some would argue, heaven's sire.

Red is gluttonous, holding every need

for only it allows, the possibility to feed.

The hues, the variegated soils,

the sly fox lava underground that boils,

the bitter cutting edges of unshaped rocks,

the vicious cold tunnels where treasure mocks,

reminds us that fragile humans are merely limbs,

helpless against wicked self-indulgent whims.

Yellow

The warmth of the universe in measured spread

melts through the night until the dark is shed.

Uplifting the spirits and creativity,

teasing away all responsibility.

Yellow is the morning sun.

Yellow comes when the damp is done,

cleansing, clearing, and even purifying

for the golden light is sweetly satisfying.

Honey bees share the splendour,

kissing soft slick petals as they meander

seeking perfect pollen sustenance

in recycled reproduction romance.

And the gentle burn of the magic ray

coming from places so far away

gives life to mountain tops, stream fed rivers,

Green fields, blue skies, and even human divas.

The Secondary – The Offspring

Green

Green, green, nature's might.

Lemon-skinned lime with an olive bite.

Apple streaks, emerald lights

of harmony and nurturing sights,

and legacies of honoured heights.

Nature cleanses so humans survive

the poison to our breathing

that growls, harshly seething

as green velvet keeps us alive.

In return we lack appreciation

and the beauty we abound in

shows a depreciation,

an almost unearthly sin.

Orange

Superb sunset and

stunning sunrise.

Orange is flamboyant,

a hostess for nature's

more excitable moments.

Desert stone takes on a fiery

festive assertion

standing proud in

Australian territory.

Fire glow and heat provider

fuelling volcanic tempers

changing adventurous rumblings

into exhibitionist explosions.

You feed red, you ignore green

but peach softens your reaction

while proud amber seeks

jewelled superficial satisfaction

and is blind to the power of blue.

Communication is on your terms,

opportunist confidence only too true.

Purple

Purple, you tell a story

with richness and splendour.

From mystic amethyst gracing

the human with glory

to the majesty of deep magenta

and the violet stained-glass placing.

Purple, you inspire the imagination.

Yet with an arrogant stance

your hues turn into deluded grandeur

fraught with pompous, cynical corruption

until deep spirituality asks for a dance

and you forgive the immature.

In fields of flowers, lilac dwells

with heather hills in competition.

The lavender evening sky stakes a claim

then sunset's royal shade preens and swells.

Dignified, it allows evening succession

from the mauve palette to dark plum fame.

The Mix – The Resulting Generation

Green to Orange

I cover the earth in:

brilliant emerald,

lengthening grassy green,

deeply darkened jade.

And, all of them fade

to a frantic fruity lime

or an olive grove glow

until the searching sea recycled,

acquiescing into aqua flow.

I acknowledge my centre:

amber glides in beaded glory,

a peach perfect gleam has a say.

So many colours for us to see

all mixing with volcanic glee.

Golden gilded gifts from a
82

centred orange furnace has

yellow flecks show their face

and in the pale heat of a fired ember

night smiles as sunrise takes its place.

Purple to Black

I look around enthralled.

Nature has provided life.

Lilac flowers breathe their scent

a pale modest muted bent.

Vibrancy arrives to ripen plums.

An evolved admired amethyst stone

processes red and blue into proven purple

in the stunning sweetness of sunsets shown.

Lovingly the pretty palette spreads,

the blended shades a symphony

where earth's dirt is dusted brown

and sable sands don't quite frown.

Then with care, ivory leaches white

allowing grey to cloud the atmosphere

to a bloated blasphemous black

before the sudden summer storms appear.

And it begins again.

The Human hand

We take a tube

and squeeze

using long thin greedy fingers.

A fisted curiosity lingers.

Rainbow colours grow by our hand

yet if we chance to step away

and just peruse the land

we see that nature has every day

shown us a better blend

to seize.

We watch

and reflect.

Where the brush had our digits curl

now slowly we choose to unfurl.

We copy what is already there,

opening our eyes wide, to see.

We comprehend our gathered fare

as nature bestows the treasured key

and kindly allows us

the grand, the very full effect.

The Haiku in Colour
(nature blending with the varied personalities of colours)

Colour me Blue

sky talk

tender blue white patches

grey grizzles

waves ripple

muddy grey to ocean blue

salt crystals

white softness

bubbles in the blue horizon

Colour me Red

passionate desire

liquid lava flow

heated destruction

warm sunshine on skin

dissipating red rays leave blemishes

the goddess Venus

distant and unforgiving planet of flames

Colour me Green

Green balance

gentle hands rejuvenate

tranquillity

palest new leaf

baby footprints expand

tangled jade scenes

green expanses

peace

lady-in-waiting

Colour me Yellow

sunshine cheerful

citrus floral stimulant

daylight vibrancy

lemon taste tickles

simulated gold on a waiting tongue

fourth finger

left hand

yellow banded vows

Colour me Purple

soft purple haze

rich flowering lavender

mystic carpet

lilac summer night

bright muted-rainbow-touched sunsets

outrageous mauve

free spirited crimson mutation

Colour me Pink

Unconditional pink

positive female energy

flirtations

passionate lovers in fuchsia

Colour me Orange

orange socialiser

dawn breaker night seducer

frantic fire

orange flames rise proud

volcano

The Cinquain in Colour
(colour meanings in action)

Red

Energetic, passionate

Stimulating, motivating, dominating

Waits with dark intensity

Power

Burgundy

Rich, sophisticated

Reigning, controlling, determining

Ambition with dignity

Regal

Crimson

Bright, beautiful

Enticing, teasing, tantalising

Emitting sexual intensity

Blood

Maroon

Strong, positive

Pondering, reflecting, wondering

Controlled thinking

Thoughtful

Blue

Conservative, predictable

Enhancing, calming, healing

Whispered wings of wisdom

Peace

Turquoise

Balance, Stability

Communicating, clarifying, recharging

Enhancer of empathy

Idealism

Navy

Conservative, compassionate

Repressing, worrying, regulating

Non-demonstrative and non-emotional entity

Corporate

Aqua

Thoughtful, honest

Refreshing, cooling, enveloping

Universally admired

Freedom

Yellow

Impatient, vibrant

Stimulating, creating, investigating

Bringing clarity to the mind

Sunshine

Orange

Sociable, playful

Rejuvenating, self-indulging, overbearing

Stimulating appetite and conversation

Optimism

Citrine

Fickle, superficial

Teasing, deceiving, retreating

Serial hopper of emotions

Unstable

Lemon

Sensitive, wary

Self-relying, cleaning, clearing

Fears the critical

Orderly

Purple

Unusual, individual

Dreaming, dignifying, meditating

Superior and regally royal

Imagination

Lavender

Fragile, sensitive

Aspiring, romancing, idolising

Muted purple power

Vulnerable

Amethyst

Concerned, decisive

Protecting, opening, evolving

A sensitive mystic soul

Humanitarian

Indigo

Intuitive, idealistic

Knowing, maintaining, conforming

Self-mastery supports structure

Contentment

The Plant Connection

Plants have long held special meanings. Each plant is individual and unique and if we listen carefully it will tell us a story of magic and medicine and of times gone by.

The Carnation

Your abundance of colour

delights the eye.

Each one a symbol

a story to apply.

Loving, admiring, rejecting.

Disdainful whilst perfecting

capricious purple, and mother love pink

is multi-faceted to make us think.

Give me white and know me pure.

Give me red full of allure.

Golden yellow may disappoint some,

and stripes may give a refusal outcome.

Encompassing plentiful and colour-varied faces,

the carnation speaks of beautiful places.

The Daffodil

So pretty, so complicated,

your meaning is almost variegated.

On your own, misfortune speaks.

Bring a bunch and you have joy,

but unrequited love seeks

new beginnings to employ.

Your delicate petals indicate rebirth.

Your ability to return suggests life eternal.

Standing in a long straight line,

buried in soft sweet earth

your chivalry can't help but shine.

reaching out from within to the external.

The Sunflower

Standing tall and on guard.

Sun lover, rich with yellow gold.

Seeds of courage carried into battle

or pounded powder to spirit hold.

You are versatile.

Your rounded shape a timekeeper,

a classically designed sun-dial,

bending as the heat hits your open face

to the delight of the harvester on hand

glowing at your offered treats.

Oil for cooking or medicinal

ailment curing, or magic feats,

or as a dye for lustreless cloth

a cooking classic cultivated for

its capability to be

so much more.

The Wisteria

I am wisteria.

I symbolise love and longevity,

bliss and tender immortality

with my gift of sensitivity.

I support, and I give

as I strive to live.

Consciousness to expand the vine

I share in abundance the purple line

of flowering blooms in their glory

allowing all to enjoy my story.

The Ash

Standing tall and strong,

the Ash sings a symbolic song.

The past, present and future blend

telling us of the rules that bend

as roots flow and spread,

when worlds join by a string, a thread.

The underworld comes first,

then middle earth with a burst.

Last to unite and to agree

is the one we too often fail to see,

the strange realm of the spiritual

badly needed to seal the mutual.

An equality in co-existence seals our fate

and helps rid us of unwanted freight.

The Ash stands tall and strong and steers man away from wrong.

Plants and the Haiku
(sharing history and meaning)

inspiring lotus

mental illuminator

cleared minds open

mandrake root

human negativity and bringer of curses

majestic poison

spellbinding charismatic oleander charm

fairies

Four-leaf-clover with fortune and fidelity

purification

grounded human emotions

parsley

rue be thy plant name

governor of sadness and depression

raspberry preserve

protective love and soil fertility offering

Ginseng enhancer

focused clarity of the mind

rainmaker pixie

eternal knowledge

archaic rich fern

liquid slow maple flow

sugar sweet longevity

pennyroyal plant

noble peace protector with majestic stature

salicylic acid and aspirin

bark baskets

willow sprigs

lily modesty

sweetness and purity of heart and soul

haughty heights

sunflower soldiers pay homage to the sun

twelve red roses

fragrant longing for love

chaste white rosebud

woman in mantilla lace splendour

sunshine warm

platonic evocation

yellow rose

mixed coloured buds

rose spawned emotions

taste of maybes

heathered lavender

gothic tales span wild solitary moors

114

tree roots

blood blackened striped veins

Mother Earth

Shadowed darkness

Elm markers repulse

Tainted woods

temperance

true representation

azalea modesty

Plants and the Cinquain

Knowledge

Ancient, smooth

Writing, wishing, replacing

Grained surface word carrier

Beech

Paradox

Powerful, deceptive

Stimulating, sedating, contradicting

Cat magic and spell maker

Catnip

Leaves

Three, four

Balancing, succeeding, protecting

Luck bringer and fairy viewer

Clover

Divination

Chaotic, random

Lusting, loving, repelling

Fertile five pretty petals

Hibiscus

Prophetic

Clumsy, awkward

Strengthening, healing, protecting

Inferring by astral projection

Mugwort

Catalyst

Magic, sacred

Hunting, exorcising, fertilising

Loved by Druids

Mistletoe

Flute

Flexible, musical

Expanding, budding, symbolising

Music making stalks

Reed

Tree

Versatile, dominant

Conducting, storing, growing

Earth elemental bargain

Spruce

Passion

Symbolic, lucky

Loving, tempting, rewarding

Creating love spells

Strawberry

Potion

Strong, youthful

Loving, energising, boosting

Druid power plant

Vervain

Faith

Shy, peaceful

Retiring, wishing, healing

Hiding behind the larger picture

Violet

Manners

Cultured, spellbinder

Stabilising, purifying, invoking

Safety in an unstable environment

Waterlily

Psychic

Dangerous, poisonous

Protecting, inducing, harming

Caller of spirits

Wormwood

Healer

Cool, protective

Soothing, calming, refreshing

Breaker of hexes

Wintergreen

Herb

Strong, pure

Healing, regenerating, aiding

Sealer of wounds

Bloodroot

Cleanser

Healthy, Healing

Exorcising, protecting, anti-thieving

Curbing poisons and disease spread

Juniper

Treasure

Hidden, Chaste

Enduring, protecting, adapting,

Environmental water storage

Cactus

Useful

Versatile, protective

Hex-breaking, growing, wishing

Fortune and safety

Bamboo

Wisdom

Open-minded, experienced

Curing, protecting, long-living

Basket maker and spiritual protector

Willow

Ceremonial

Generous, provident

Cleansing, prospering, healing

Amulets and medicinal bundles

Cedar

Till next time, be kind to plants, treasure them because they have magic, Barb

From the Author

If you have read this far then you have finished reading Emotions in Evolution, the second book in a poetic trilogy. Both books are reflections on life as we journey through trials and tribulations. The trilogy has been a pet project of mine and I would love your feedback.

I know how hard it is to choose what we read simply on the look of a cover and a brief outline. For this reason and for your reading pleasure, I have enclosed the beginning chapters of the first novel in my series. **Unexpected Obsession** is **Book 1** in **The Unexpected Series**. I have, in the hope that you like it enough to read it, also enclosed the first chapters of the second book. **Unexpected Obsession** is currently under re-edit and should be out December 2018. **Unexpected Passion** still has some way to go but with some work and some luck should be released early 2019 as will my psychological/paranormal thriller **The Narrow Hallway**. If you like the chapters and have some input to offer, please feel free to let know (see below).

I am so grateful you have taken the time and spent money on something I have written. Would you please consider leaving a review? Be as honest as you wish. I learn from your words, your thoughts and ideas. For Indie authors, reviews can make the difference between success and financial solvency or nothing. Word of mouth is an author's best friend.

Just a brief word and a rating left at Amazon will truly make that difference.

Thank you,

Barbara Strickland.

I don't have a newsletter but will post news and updates through my website. Important news will be shared through my Amorina Rose's blog (found on the home page). Please subscribe to my blog as I would love to hear from you. I also have a contact email attached to my official website:

www.brstrickland.com

Contact me: barb@brstrickland.com or follow me at:

Amorina Rose's blog at www.brstrickland.com

www.goodreads.com

Amazon.com

Facebook

Twitter

Pinterest

Instagram

Books

Unexpected Obsession (The Unexpected Series Book 1)

Emotions in Eruptions (A poetic journey through life)

Emotions in Evolution (The emotional journey continues)

TBA

Emotions in Existence (The emotional journey lasts forever}

The Narrow Hallway (a psychological and paranormal thriller stand-alone)

Unexpected Passion (The Unexpected Series Book 2)

Unexpected Christmas Gathering (The Unexpected Series, Book 3)

Unexpected Desire (The Unexpected Series Book 4)

Unexpected Summer Heat (The Unexpected Series Book 5)

Unexpected Outcomes (The Unexpected Series, Book 6)

Green Mists (a science fiction stand-alone romance)

Memories of the Heart (memoirs with a twist)

Lance finds Home (a children's book)

About the author

I'm an Aussie with an Italian heritage. The warmth and beauty of both cultures has always inspired me, and I thought mixing it all together and adding a few other cultures in my books would be fun. I grew up in a multi-cultural environment with a dream to speak as many languages as possible, travel till there is no more to be seen, and own a dog and cat and have space for them both. I have a degree in teaching, three children and some amazing grandchildren and love reading, reading and more reading.

<u>Unexpected Obsession</u>
(The novel is undergoing a re-edit, to be finished December 2018)
<u>The Unexpected Series Book 1</u>

Chapter 1

THE SCRAPE OF the chair on the cream tiles unnerved her. The noise was an intrusion reminding her, she was unwanted here. She sat down anyway. If Lia hadn't been internally shaking from fear, she thought, she might have laughed at the two people battling to deal with her audacity, and she might have felt a little embarrassed at her behaviour.

"What the devil are you doing here? You can't be serious!" Domenico was spitting enough fire to make a dragon proud. His height, the dark eyes intense and glaring, and the tight mouth were enough on their own to make her nervous. The quiet menace in his voice was an unwanted extra. Angelia looked searchingly at the man in front of her. The gangly sixteen-year old with the pretty-boy looks had disappeared. His place was taken by a very tall and well-built stranger. The dark close to black hair was just short of military precision. Domenico's face was close shaven. The man looked like he had stepped out of a Hollywood golden era, in his black suit (designer label of course), pristine white shirt, and bold red tie. Even the black leather shoes were immaculate.

Nothing here existed of the boy, the one her seven-year-old-self had worshipped. He had towered over her, a closed, aloof scowling giant to her smaller self. Somehow, she had gotten through the barriers to win his affection. Not once had she feared him. At twenty-eight years of age her height had caught up but not enough to stop her feeling just a little afraid of the man he had become. This time around those barriers were chillingly impregnable.

She swallowed and concentrated on the couple. They on the other hand, did not seem so different. Twenty years had only aged them. Gina looked so much like Papa that Lia felt a stab at her heart. Gina had been Papa's step-sister. Nonno had remarried after Nonna Maria died. Nonna Enza had a child, a scandal in the family because she hadn't been married and no-one knew who the father was. Papa had told Lia that Nonna Enza had been related in some fashion and hence he and Gina had looked so alike it had cemented a strong sibling relationship. Gina, Papa had told Lia, had always believed Antonio to be a surprise her parents had brought home just for her. He had been her baby, not just her little step-brother. Funny, Lia thought as an unpleasant trickle of cold slid along her spine, how one terrible moment in the past had shattered so many relationships, so many lives.

"Are you listening? What the hell are you doing here?"

"I rang first, remember?" She met his gaze bravely, aware that flinching would give him the upper hand.

"Domenico, you told her not to come? Why is she here?" Gina clutched at her heart. Unsteady in her gait, Gina leaned against the wall as she spoke. Domenico moved swiftly. He reached his mother before she lost her balance. He growled at Angelia. It made her feel sick inside. Someone else stood there watching, a thoughtful look on his face. Recognising her Uncle Lucio, Lia braced herself for another emotional outburst. Lucio remained quiet. His head tilted in surprise, but he still managed to rein in his expression enough to puzzle her. She remembered a different man, one of quick action, not this silent bystander who seemed out of place in his own home.

"You're my family. I don't need an invitation. I have every right to be here." She threw the letter she had written to them a scarce few months ago on the table. It had been returned unopened, unread just like all the other letters her father had sent to his sister over the years. "Since there is obviously something wrong with the Italian postal service, I thought I'd deliver the letter, my letter, to you in person. Funny thing though, it was marked return to sender from right here in Catania. Strange isn't it? Never mind. I have it here now. You know the letter I mean, the one about my father's accident. The one that told you he died." She released the bit of air that she had been holding in. The sound was loud in her ears. She looked away, focusing on the apartment; determined Domenico would not rattle her. It looked familiar, spotless from floor to ceiling, and the dining table was the same, a dark rich mahogany. Uncle Lucio had made it himself, and that little bit of knowledge from so long ago gave her confidence, despite the looming presence making her heart beat faster.

"Is this how people in Australia behave? They walk into someone's home, unannounced, and uninvited?"

She turned away from staring at the older man, distracted by the younger one's harsh tone. She hid her shaking hands behind her back, glad he was a distance from her. Over near the cream leather lounge where he had placed his mother, the aura he exuded was easier to handle. The lounge, another thing she remembered. Idly she mused that good pieces were pieces you kept. So why then had her aunt been so willing to throw away a lifetime of memories of the only family she had? Surely people mattered more than things?

"I told you on the phone we knew, wasn't that enough? Your father is dead..." Domenico stopped short as his mother let out an anguished moan. His face hardened further. "I'll say this in your language Angelia, in English so there is no misunderstanding. We don't need to know any more about him or you. Naturally we sympathise but that's as far as it goes. We aren't interested in any other letters and we aren't interested in you."

"Well, isn't that too fucking bad!" Lia muttered back, making sure he could see her mouth enunciating English words. If Domenico was fluent, and he was with that almost perfect pronunciation, then she was sure he would lip read her correctly. His mouth tightened, and she smiled, a little smug at his understanding. He was fucking with her brain. Speaking to her in English as if she was a stranger, making her feel like an outsider. *Not in this lifetime, dickhead.* "I thought my aunt," she replied, in Italian and with volume, enunciating each word carefully, "might need a sympathetic ear. After all, he was the only family she had left."

"Listen to me, little girl." Gina's snarl reverberated as pain in Lia's heart, the heart searching to find the aunt she remembered. Gina was still a pretty woman despite the lines of discord marring her forehead. Her uncoloured hair needed a trim but otherwise suited her. Some women looked good going grey and Gina was one of them. "I don't need or want you here. How I feel is my business, so get out. Go home!"

The pain at Gina's obvious lack of regard or affection changed to fear at the paleness of her aunt's face, at the veins now prominent in the forehead, shiny and slick with moisture, and at the obvious breathing difficulties. A panic attack, Lia thought. Domenico was whispering calming words, but his dark eyes were turned on Lia, fierce and narrowed. None of this was going to plan. What had she expected? In her peripheral vision she saw her uncle make a move towards Gina. He halted at the vicious look his son gave him. Lia swallowed and bit the inside of her cheek, willing herself to keep still. *God there was so much happening here!* The words pounded in Lia's head. If she moved, they would see her fear and she couldn't allow that.

The letters were supposed to explain. Over the years her Papa had written his sister about everything in their lives, good and bad. She had thought to convince her aunt to read them. She hadn't thought it through. Lia hadn't realised how fragile Gina was in body. Never a large woman, she was now a small frame of breakable bones. Lia bit down on her lip with despair at the thought that not even her brother's death could dent the bitterness and hatred emanating from Gina.

"You heard her! Get out!" Domenico's voice was a bombardment. His attention on her lip worse somehow. She stopped biting on it, perturbed by the sharp gaze. "And you," Domenico barked in Italian without turning his head to his father, "go get her medication, or has this one dazzled you with her looks the way her slut of a mother did."

His continued focus on her mouth was uncomfortable. His satisfaction at this was on his face but he had miscalculated with his words. Even if he had reason to say what he did, where Marissa was concerned, it was cruel, an unnecessary taunt. It touched a raw nerve and gave purpose and strength back to Lia.

"I'm staying even if I have to sleep on the floor." Lia stood up and walked over to where she had placed her bags. She picked up her back pack from where it rested on the ground, pulled out a plastic bag and turned to face her aunt. "This has every letter my father wrote. I am not leaving until I see you read each, and every one of them. He loved you. He needed you, not your punishment. I know your reasons were good ones. They belong in the past. It may be too late for him; it's not too late for me to do this for him. You are going to read every word and then I'll go. Mark my words, you will read them. He deserves to be remembered." Lia tilted her head, letting her expression show her determination.

"Who do you think you're dealing with?" Domenico was suddenly standing in front of her. His eyes had darkened to a black abyss holding her own, prisoner. The intimidating look, the same one he had given her on opening the door strengthened her resolve. Lia held her ground, staring straight into the void. No doubt this same scenario would be repeated. She shrugged as if she hadn't a care in the world and turned away. The relief to be away from that unyielding stare nearly buckled her knees. "You're just a rude, arrogant little bitch!" His voice was a low hiss behind her, his tone menacing, the English words cold.

"It's obvious we are related then," she replied in Italian. "Although I would think arsehole suits you much better. It's more masculine." She turned and held that last word just long enough to let him know she whole-heartedly doubted the latter. Smiling inwardly, she reflected his tirade was quite mild compared to the words he might have used in his own language. That was the beauty of the Italian language, she thought, letting herself be distanced from the scene in front of her for a moment, to recoup. Swearing and name-calling were extremely creative. His reply was a supercilious sneer, annoying Lia further. She didn't censor what came next. "Perhaps, a rude arrogant bastard is more apt? Bastard, being the operative word, I'd imagine." Her words were beneath her. The gasp from her aunt testified to just how much that was true. She deserved the terrifying anger she glimpsed in Domenico before his face smoothed over.

His body was still coiled tight. Lia felt his physical battle to relax his shoulders before giving her a dismissive look. Her own body remained tense with shame. Her retort had been nasty. This wasn't her way. She wanted to erase her words but didn't know how and backing down was not an option. Fortunately, she had an unexpected reprieve from the one other person who might also have taken offence at her words.

"Leave her alone. This is my house and I say she can stay."

"Well, of course old man, you would come to her rescue. You fucked her mother in this very home, so what now? The daughter?"

Lia cringed at the crude, spiteful way Domenico had chosen to re-direct his anger at her. Lucio stood resolute, not even a blink. Lia found it painful to watch, especially since her aunt seemed unmoved by this interchange. The skin of her face though was paler, almost grey. Not the steely hue of her thick hair, but a pasty looking imitation.

"Take your mother to her room. She needs her pills and to lie down. Keep your opinions to yourself. I repeat – this is my house." His voice was quiet, yet it had an underlying strength. Not surprisingly,

Domenico did as he was asked. Lia let go of the breath she was holding. Her chest no longer restricted, she turned her eyes to Lucio.

"Thank you! I'm so sorry."

"This is a very complicated household. My son took it easy on you. Next time he won't be as pleasant." She made a rude sound and he laughed. "Believe me, he let you off lightly. He is very possessive and very protective where his mother is concerned, and he was worried about her. Me, he doesn't care too much for."

Despite the silver flecks in his hair, Lucio was still an exceptionally handsome man. The bone structure heralded antiquity. A strong jaw line and an almost perfectly, oval shaped face was reminiscent of statues of Roman gods. He was taller, too, than many Italian men, about half a head under six feet, and had an air of confidence, at least when his son's piercing gaze wasn't aimed at him. His son, Lia suspected, never lost that arrogant tilt of eyebrows. Yes. Lucio was very good-looking. So was his son. Even more so, because whilst Domenico had that same facial structure, he also had a look of Gina in the bone structure around his eyes, eyes dark like the most decadent chocolate, with long lashes most women would envy. Her father had the same eyes and so did she. Without them she would have been a clone of Marissa, her mother.

"You're different to what I expected." Lia narrowed her gaze to focus on Lucio. The cocky self-assuredness she remembered was missing. Even as a child she had noted, his confidence in his appeal as a male, in his ability to charm.

"More charming?"

She couldn't help indulging his use of that word with a small laugh. He shrugged self-deprecatingly. Lia could see sadness in those eyes.

"Age softens and changes things for some. Your aunt, my wife, is a hard woman. She lost a child and did considerable damage to her leg and we both know the how and why of it, don't we?" He waited for Lia to acknowledge his words. At her nod he continued. "I think it's too late for her to change her feelings and her ways. I am telling you, so you won't be disappointed even..."

Lia waited for him to continue, realising he was mellower, more approachable as if the edge had been rubbed right off him. Back then his good looks and surety had scared her a little. "Even...?"

"Even as I am hoping you succeed. Domenico will fight you being here. Ignore him. You are welcome to stay as long as you want. I meant what I said. This is my house."

"Thank you."

"You'll be sharing a bathroom with Domenico."

Lucio's raised eyebrows made her smile. "Is he still a clean freak?"

"You're still that bright little girl, aren't you?" Lucio laughed quietly in reply. "You have a good memory, and yes he is. Everything must have a place, usually where he puts it. Don't leave a wet sink. There are paper towels to wipe the basin down. Can you cope?"

"You're enjoying this, aren't you?" She smiled wryly, pleased to see a twinkle in his eyes wiping some of the sadness away.

"It might be just what this family needs," he replied. The twinkle was replaced with a more sombre look. "Lia, Domenico is harsh and lives by rules, usually his, but he is a good person. Too strong, far too precise in expectations, yet for all that, he has never shirked family responsibility, even with me. Give him time. Now, do you want a coffee?"

She nodded again, understanding his need to shift the conversation.

"Uncle Lucio, will she be alright? She didn't look too good."

"She gets emotional and needs medication for her heart. Your aunt...your aunt is stronger than she thinks. She didn't believe you would come. Gina hates confrontations, and to be honest she has hung on to her bitterness for so long she doesn't know anything else. Seeing you is...conflicting. She loved you so much. We all did."

He turned away, heading for the kitchen. Lia frowned. Despite all she knew of the past, she found this Lucio likeable.

"Are you sure about this?"

Halting, he turned at her question. "You look shattered! Why don't you settle into your room? Stop thinking, there's plenty of time for that."

His words made her feel safe and strangely wanted. Lia walked back to her bags, picked them up and carried them to the room with a lighter heart. She would need sheets, but Lucio was already there, handing her towels and linen before disappearing. He moved gracefully, a trait she had noticed in Domenico who had prowled the room like a cat. Lia sat on the bed, wondering again what she had got herself into, because the reality was not just this room. It comprised dinner, lunch, breakfast, using the bathroom, sleeping and doing all this in a house where she wasn't wanted.

Lucio came back with coffee. He had also thoughtfully prepared a tray containing biscuits, cheese and olives. He was quiet, unobtrusive as he put the things he carried on the small bedside table. The sadness was back in his eyes.

"I've brought you a spare set of keys." Pausing he held her eyes. "They will fight you. Just ignore them and treat this as your home. Eat when we eat. Gina will feed you. It is her way and it might provide an avenue for discussion, or not." He shrugged, looking self-conscious at Lia's intent stare. "She cooks for me, washes and irons my clothes despite the fact we haven't shared much else for twenty years, and she will do the same for you and hate you just as much. She's like that."

"Why? Why are you really allowing this?

"I owe Antonio. He was a good man, one of the best. He was my friend not just my brother-in-law. The past is a heavy burden at this age. Maybe you are the key to change. I am so tired of the cold. Today for the first time I felt a little warmth. You have brought the sun."

"Solare," she whispered at his retreating back. That had been his word for her back then, teasing her that she was sunshine. She sat for a long time after he left. Dinner that evening was not pleasant, but she stayed, refusing to be baited by either mother or son.

Chapter 2

GINA WOULD play old records on an antiquated record player as she did the housework, and sometimes she would sing. Her voice was soft and sweet and unexpected from someone who had seemingly forgotten to smile. The first morning Lia sang along was the first time she felt Gina really saw her and not her mother, not Marissa. It wasn't hard to feel emotion and put it into the singing, after a fortnight of being ignored except in the evenings when Lucio returned from work. The ignoring did have its merits though. Shivering, even now a week later, she recalled the encounter with Domenico. It had almost sent her running home.

"Don't you know to knock?"

"This is my home, not yours, remember?"

"What do you want?"

"To give you a friendly word of warning, my dear sweet little cousin."

"Step-cousin more like it, and the little bit of blood we share is about two generations removed, thank you very much. Not that it makes a difference. Either way I'm pretty sure, your family welcome would still be underwhelming." Lia had barely restrained the smirk. Her fear of starting something held her in check and only for her aunt's sake.

"I'm watching you. I'm not my father to be swayed by looks."

His gaze had moved insolently from the pale pink polished toe nails and bare feet and slowly up, stopping only when he reached her mouth. She had read too many books to let her teeth bite down on her bottom lip. The temptation was strong; it was an instinctive action. He made her uneasy, and not because he made her feel unwelcome. She wasn't sure she needed or wanted to know the reason. It was enough she understood it was his intention to make her uncomfortable. His striking presence was unsettling. Looks and personality, however, could be so at odds. She remained silent but didn't look away.

"My mother has been through too much in her life. Hurt her in any fashion and I'll make you sorry in ways you can't possibly imagine. I won't let a stronza like you contaminate the air around her."

"So, you can use the Italian language when it suits you. You're the only one doing the hurting from where I sit. I don't want to hurt anyone."

"Forgive my foolish assumption. It couldn't be because your behaviour in forcing yourself on us suggests no morals or manners."

"Thanks for the little chat. I think the only stronzo here is you. It's long overdue for you to put a sock in it. I've been trying to be polite, avoid arguments, and show you I do have manners!"

His jaw tightened in disdainful and dismissive amusement. "A sock? Is this some clever Australianism you are imparting on my poor, ignorant brain?"

His tone was polite and yet it flowed with arrogance. How did he manage that? How did he manage to make her feel stupid? "Yes, I said sock. To be exact I said put a sock in it. So, it seems you are not familiar with this particular expression. I'm surprised, as I have been quite impressed at your command of English. I can only surmise you had an excellent teacher."

Domenico just lifted the one eyebrow and waited; complete distaste for her all too evident.

"How can I explain?" Lia was close to saturation point. If he wasn't making nasty comments, he acted as if she didn't exist and spoke around her. Domenico presumed and accused, and continually taunted, despite her best efforts to be friendly, to be nice and to find her way back to the warmth and affection that had existed in the past. She suspected he knew that and took pleasure in the opposite. Perhaps what she wanted was unrealistic in these early days. Right now, though, her anger was too far gone to listen to reason.

She turned in her chair and used the wheels to push away from the desk until she was closer to him. "I said, put a sock in it, right here." Lia stretched over as she spoke and grabbed his crotch and twisted. "A sock in here will ensure that everyone understands how big a dick you actually are, not have, but are. Although I need to stress, if your dick is as pathetic as your behaviour, then it too, might be an issue, a small one but an issue."

The look on his face was priceless; her enjoyment short-lived. Domenico grabbed her wrist, forcing her hand to envelop him, a 'him', or 'it' that was a little bigger and harder than she needed to know. It throbbed. She squirmed. A feeling she couldn't even think about caused her hand to flicker against him and he, it, the thing she couldn't give a name to, jerked against her fingers. For a split second she pushed against him slowly, curiously fascinated by the way it seemed to shape itself to her hand, and the way it felt, hard and soft at the same time. Common sense and reality reared, snapping her to attention. Lia tried to pull away.

"You think you are so smart! You foolish little girl! You have no idea what you're up against. Don't ever touch me again unless you're invited, or you will get so much more than you bargained for." Domenico gave her a smug look as the colour rose from her neck to the roots of her hair.

She heard herself make a small clicking sound as she struggled to prevent the grimace her face was pursuing as she felt the embarrassing warmth pervade her cheeks. Lia tried harder to tug her hand away. He just pressed it tighter against his body. She couldn't look at him. "You already seem to have the more. Feels good, doesn't it? Or at least it does to me. I guess my dick doesn't discriminate as well as I do."

Her anger spiked. Lia squeezed and twisted hard. She wanted to hurt. Lia heard the hitch in Domenico's breathing as he tightened his grip on her wrist so cruelly she had to open her hand. He was now hurting her. But, it was worth it. He had expected her to fight him but not attack again and he hadn't been ready. She looked up in satisfaction only to have that look die under the blaze of heat in his eyes.

"Well, well, well, it seems to me you have quite a bit of your mother in you, don't you? Like playing with dicks, do we?"

"I don't know about playing, but in your case 'dick' is the point I was trying to make." She tried to pull away. He exerted even more pressure to keep her hand in place.

"What a clever play on words. Don't look so surprised. I did have very good teachers. Good enough to know you need to widen your vocabulary. You do seem to enjoy the word 'dick'. I prefer cock myself."

The flame of heat in his eyes contrasted sharply with the coldness in his voice. Keeping her hand in his grasp he moved it to brush the solid length in a sweeping motion. His use of the word cock had shocked her. The inappropriateness was distracting, and it gave him control. Instinctively her fingers spread to cover him. In reaction his cock jerked against her hand again. The feeling it stirred created an odd connection to the more intimate parts of her body.

Lia felt sick. She glared at the face sculpted in stone. Domenico let her go. She wiped her hand ruthlessly on her jeans. The stone face cracked a little with a small *smug laugh before it closed off again with an indifference that made her want to hit him. Something in his gaze though, made her wary. Lia was smart enough to recognise she was in over her head.*

"That was disgusting, you are disgusting!" she muttered, completely flustered and furious and not at all able to understand a situation he had turned around so easily to his advantage. How had he gained the upper hand?

"Really? I fucking loved it. Want me to return the favour? It might add a whole new dimension to our relationship."

"What a total arsehole you are!"

"Why? Because I won 'this round'? I always win. If you don't like it, leave." Nico walked out, leaving her shaken and puzzled, and dismayed at the fact that she had referred to him as Nico even if it occurred in her mind. Why that small fact bothered her the most, considering the entire situation, was far too complex to contemplate.

The sound of her aunt's voice brought her back to the present.

"Back from the land of the fairies, are we? So, did he teach you the songs?"

Words, and not just a look or semi-growl, were a decided improvement despite the tone. Lia schooled her features to hide her excitement. She looked up from her computer where she sat every morning.

"Yes. Or sometimes it would be Mama, especially when she was sick. It helped her pass the time."

"Always the old songs, he liked the old songs, especially this one. Ha! *Calabria Mia* of all things!" Gina huffed, ignoring any mention of Lia's mother.

Lia had hoped her willingness to help around the house and with the cooking had softened Gina a little, but her aunt was not an easy person to get through to. "It's what it represented. Sicily, Calabria, in the end they all were Italians who'd left their homes, left their families. They were lonely for those things. Please read his letters," Lia asked, as she did every day, not ashamed of the plea in her voice.

"So determined!" Gina huffed again and turned away.

"Yes. You owe it to your brother."

"I don't owe anybody anything. I did nothing, it was done to me, remember? I am sure you know the story, you seem to know everything." She had her back to Lia. She went quiet and then turned slowly to glance slyly at Lia. "Tell me, little girl, will you tell me about the nightmares if I do read one?"

"Why?" It took all of Lia's self-control not to react to the sudden change in conversation.

"I'm curious about you. I don't remember you as such a rude child and I wondered maybe if guilt was manifesting itself. It can't be easy to be where you are; so obviously unwanted."

Lia shut down her computer and tried hard not to let the hurt show. So what if she wasn't the little girl adored by her aunt? There were worse things in life. Things like losing both parents. Lia stood and walked slowly forward stopping directly in front of Gina.

"You're so determined to be the wicked, hateful witch, aren't you? Here's your chance to gloat. It's true. It's all about guilt. Too bad it's not quite the way you might imagine." Lia lifted her arms to the back of her dress, unzipped it and slowly turned her body so Gina had a good view of her back. She eased the dress aside so that Gina could follow the unsightly-looking pink line around to the front of her body. She heard Gina's surprised indrawn breath and cringed a little. Lia didn't want pity. Then again, pity was an honest emotion, and Lia wasn't too proud to take whatever she could get.

"You were there? In the car? No one told us."

"Does it matter? It doesn't make my father less dead, does it, or me, any less guilty for surviving?" A gasp followed, a tangible silence. Lia used the opportunity to pull the blue fabric back up. She almost winced when soft hands took over sliding the zip.

"How?"

Lia turned and stared at her aunt, debating the wisdom of revealing so much. The details weren't pleasant. Did Gina need the reality of the accident? Would it make her more amiable, more likely to remember the little brother she once adored? What if Lia could reach both the loving aunt and her father's sister? Lia had to try, so she hoped her smile didn't reflect the bitterness she felt. "What do you want to know?"

***

A long-time later Lia stood, left the kitchen and came back to the table to place the first letter down in front of the tear-stained face of an old woman. Lia found the letter untouched when she returned an hour later from her room. Her aunt wasn't in the apartment; Lia hadn't heard her leave. She sat down and stared at the envelope as if waiting for an answer. *There was always tomorrow and the next day. It's not like I have to get back for work. Most of it is online.* Lia was restless. It wouldn't help her win this war of nerves. If she was to be honest, she was very disappointed in everything about this trip, at least where her family were concerned.

At the beginning she had been unsure about coming. Lia had thought Papa was trying to force things. Slowly Lia had come around. Why have families if you let them fall apart? Why then did people bother having children? Families were important; they sustained you. Sometimes things happened; it was the nature of people. Lia understood things could bring pain, but families forgave. Living in bitterness wasn't the answer. Where was the Gina she remembered, the affectionate sister, the loving aunt who had wanted a little girl just like Angelia? That woman had demonstrated an amazing capacity to feel.

Lia sighed. Her aunt was right. The damage had been done to Gina, and despite her own brother's death Gina didn't know how to let go of that. Lia wanted the affection back. She needed it. Papa had been right to want this for her. Even with all the angst, a companionship had developed between them. Gina could deny it till she was blue in the face, but Lia felt it growing. She wanted to stay. She wanted a little of that first time here so many years ago, and she wanted her superhero. She laughed at herself. *Domenico was not going to be an easy conquest.*

Things were hard enough with her aunt. Lia's shoulders shrugged dismissively. *Time to be more positive.* The boy had been so annoyed with her persistence in following him around. And then, Domenico had given in. All it had taken was for the seven-year-old Lia to put her hand in his to cross the road. He had raised those dark brows and she had smiled, not at all rebuffed by his scowl. "*Have it your way then.*" She had smiled again at his answer. He proceeded to indulge her from that day despite the teasing of his friends. That boy was still there surely even if buried in the layers of the man. Lia had patience, and she reminded herself she was a strategic planner. Her aunt was the key to harmony.

Maybe another way was possible to break down the barriers between them, a simpler way that might also ease the boredom of the wait. Lia needed to do some shopping for the project spinning around in her head.

***

The pattern she had chosen was simple but interesting, to encourage interaction. Pinning the squares together to make rows was a slow procedure, as the seams had to be exact. It had the desired outcome; too strong-willed to ask questions, by the end of the week Gina had stopped resisting the lure of brightly coloured fabric joining Lia at the table, quietly observing, never uttering a word and never picking up the letter that waited there every day. The battle of wills, a gentle lull, spoiled only when Domenico came home for lunch. If looks could kill Lia would have shrivelled up weeks ago.

This morning was different. Last night Gina had come in and soothed her when she had dreamt of the accident, and then waited until Lia had fallen asleep again. Now, Gina had picked up the pieces of material to touch them, the dressmaker in her unable to stop the need. When Gina had replaced the pieces on the table, Lia swallowed, almost afraid to breathe, as the rustle of paper was heard. She continued sewing and didn't look up once until her aunt put the letter down and silently shuffled away.

Lia picked it up and took it to her room and placed it in the plastic bag with the others. She took another one out before returning the bag to the dresser drawer. Neither woman had spoken about the previous night, yet something had changed. Tomorrow, the second letter would be on the table waiting for Gina, just as the next time the memories woke Lia, a hand would be there to chase away the darkness. *I won't make more of this than it is*, Lia kept telling herself.

***

Gina had read a letter a day now for over a week. She had also become quite vocal about the quilt Lia was creating. No other more normal conversation occurred yet the feeling of companionship continued to flourish. This morning they had baked. Later they had enjoyed the cake with coffee before setting up the sewing machine. When the phone rang, and Gina pointedly looked at Lia, she struggled not to roll her eyes at her aunt. Domenico always rang at this time.

"Pronto"

"Where's my mother?" The voice was curt, dismissive and distinctly annoyed. Lia thought of it as his trifecta tone, three winning ways to piss off Lia. She wondered what he would think of that little piece of Australianism. *There go my good intentions.* Gina would get her performance.

"Well hello to you too and thanks for asking, and yes I am well. What can I do for you?" Any conversation they had was always conducted in English. He was determined to make her feel distanced from the family, from the whole country. Lia found it amusing.

"Leave Italy but put my mother on the phone first."

Lia held the phone towards Gina.

"Tell him I'm busy and he can talk to you." Lia bit the inside of her cheek at her aunt's little game.

"She can't talk right now. Can I take a message?" Lia smiled, knowing exactly how irate he'd be at Lia's saccharine sweet tone, and his mother's behaviour. Lia and Nico both knew Gina received some sort of perverse pleasure from their confrontations even if conducted in a foreign language. Neither one though was prepared to back off. The result as usual was an unpleasant conversation with Domenico.

"I'll tell her," Lia said very politely. "Please do enjoy the rest of your day."

"Why, have you packed your bags?"

"Go fuck yourself."

"Such beautiful manners. You know, as a matter of fact, I was just about to follow that suggestion, but not on my own."

"You're a pig." With those words she slammed the phone down. She didn't miss the glimpse of humour on the normally dour face before her aunt swiftly looked away. "He's not coming home for lunch and won't be home tonight either."

"Probably Francesca again!" Gina puffed her displeasure.

It hadn't taken Lia long to learn Francesca was not liked. Having met her briefly, Lia understood perfectly. Francesca was a beautiful, egotistical bitch.

"Intelligent enough when she can get past herself. Too bad that doesn't happen often. My Nico should know better, even if her father is an important man..." Gina stopped, Lia surmised, on realising she was actually making conversation.

"They deserve each other. They're both arrogant arseholes!" Lia looked up suddenly, realising she spoken out loud. The pleasant atmosphere had just evaporated. Lia could see it reflected in the distortion of features on Gina's face.

"Because I read the letters you think you have rights now, to criticise my son and his choice of partner?"

"No, I'm sorry. I didn't mean to say anything."

"Yes you did. You don't like my son. I'll admit he isn't very nice to you. Coming here with an agenda negated winning a popularity contest, especially since no thought was given to whom you may hurt or impose on, correct?" Gina didn't wait for a reply. "He may be difficult at times. Don't pull that face. He is my son so you, you need to keep your mouth shut. I don't care what he says to you or about you, but I do care what you say *about* him. Not to him but about him, so be very careful, Angelia, very careful."

"That isn't fair Aunt Gina. He is so..."

"Don't!"

"But..."

"I said, don't! Let me finish reading and then another coffee and you can tell me more about Sydney."

Lia knew she would lose the little ground she had gained if she protested. She continued working in silence while her aunt went back to the letter. *There was always tomorrow. Si, domani!* Lia sighed. She seemed to be repeating the tomorrow phrase constantly, almost as often as she sighed these days. Her determination was faltering. Domenico had that effect. She kept looking for the hero of years ago and instead kept slamming up against the sharp, hard planes of a man who left the bathroom spotless and smelling expensive, exclusive and so excluding where she was concerned.

She understood he upset her equilibrium with his refusal to accept her back into the family fold. Their constant bickering shrouded something cavernous. At times an insidious element celebrated his rejection. Lia thought of it as an unexpected and complicated puzzle piece. She kept her eyes on the fabric in her hands.

***

"Fuck!" Domenico slammed the phone down on his desk in his office on the other side of the city. Something about her grated in a way he couldn't ignore. She had just walked in like she owned the place, stirring up emotions best forgotten. As if, he thought, his mother hadn't been hurt enough already with the events of the past, they now had a living reminder. In every movement, every look, the way she held her head he saw Marissa come to life, except for the eyes. Marissa's had been a sea green and her hair a touch lighter. Even so, the resemblance was uncanny and all of it pissed him off.

However, Lia's mouth annoyed him the most. The things she came out with, the language despite the innocence of that perfect face. Those little comments about his being a mamma's boy because he still lived at home were wearing thin. Lia pronounced it *mama*, an Australian idiosyncrasy that further grated on his nerves. Although he had to admit, he did incite her at every opportunity; a perverse entertainment. Domenico enjoyed making her miserable, especially since he couldn't forget the way she had stood up to him that day. A part of him had applauded her recklessness. At the same time, he wanted to squash her like a fly. She had actually touched his dick. He had never felt such anger or such a heated response. He still didn't know how he managed to stay in control of both his temper and his body. Her defiance had aroused him, had unleashed a heat he had not thought possible. It stilled burned. *That one moment when she had leaned into his rigid cock, her hand shaping...fuck her.* Why couldn't she take the hints and go back to Australia? He gave them out often enough.

Of course, the old man rushed in to defend her at every opportunity. He was eating the attention up. Who knew what went on in his mind, fawning all over her and her sweet little ways? Why was his mother being so quiet about it all? After the initial outbursts she hadn't said much at all.

He adored his mother. She'd always made him feel safe, and powerful. Not once had she complained when he needed his room a certain way, his things arranged in a certain order.

"Mamma, they have to go back exactly like this."

His father on the other hand...Nico knew the old man resented finding himself having to marry Gina. He could accept those feelings. They had certain logic. Being made to take on a wife and child for propriety couldn't have been easy. That Lucio couldn't accept Domenico's inability to fit the image in Lucio's mind of what a *son* should be was unforgivable. Now Lia had brought the whole situation to the forefront again, just by existing. His whole routine at home was thrown out.

"I don't get it." He paced around the room as he spoke and then came back to stop directly in front of his mother. "Has she become your little pet?"

"Domenico, Nico, that's not exactly a kind way to refer to the girl," she replied, not hiding her amusement at his rant.

"Well, now you're reading the letters, letting her play with your sewing machine and having cosy little meetings at the kitchen table. What the hell Ma?"

"She entertains me. She is such a determined little thing and she has some right on her side."

"What's the matter Ma? And don't shake that head at me!"

"She makes me feel lonely and confused but..."

"That's it, she has to go."

"No, you don't understand. What I mean is, she is making me see how narrow my life is and..."

"I'm not enough? Do I make it too much with my ways?"

"Nico, I enjoy doing things for you. You know that."

"No, I ask too much. I demand too much! The bitch is right. I should have my own place."

"Nico, stop! I'll admit you can be challenging," she had said with that wide smile and her eyes radiating love and warmth. "It's hard to explain, but she fills a void. In some ways she isn't so different to you, you know. She likes things clean and tidy, and she helps me willingly. I like it...I..."

"It's an act, this being so helpful. Come on, Ma. She has an agenda, a twisted one that justifies forcing herself on us."

"No, it's her. Can you let me talk?" He had nodded, if unwillingly and she had continued. "She is a sharer, of her heart and maybe a little of her soul, she has...I can't explain but she brings the sun. Solare, you father would say when she was little. Don't pout, my son. It's not like we have to admit any of this to her."

"No, she looks too much like Marissa not to have some of her nature. I don't want her here, and if she hurts you in any way...."

"You and I, Nico, have never needed anybody else. Maybe that's not right. We do need others. Leave her alone. I'm not asking you to be nice to her."

"I love you Mamma, so whatever makes you happy. You need to know I don't like it. I don't like her!"

"You did once."

"She was a child then, sweet, not this bitch with letter issues."

"Domenico, he was my brother. He was my family. Leave her alone, for me."

"Fuck!" he growled back in the present. He turned to face the woman in his office.

"Did you lock the door after Ivana left? Good girl," he said, tracing a finger from her cheek to the full red lips when she nodded. He inserted his finger and she was quick to suck on it. His cock jerked in response. "And what else did you do?" In reply Francesca dangled a black lace thong. He took it and tossed it to the floor. Tangling his hands in the back of her long thick hair, he pushed her face down towards his desk. Still holding her hair, he halted so she was just hovering, a breath away from the solid timber. "Do you see all my files, my pens, how nicely they are laid out?" He pulled on her hair and she nodded. "Good, now remember no matter what I don't want any disruption to my desk. I have work to do later."

With those words he pushed her head down so her forehead was on the surface of the desk. He placed her hands flat above her head over the files he was working on. "Now don't move" he ordered. He hitched up her skirt, shoving his knee between her legs, pushing her thighs apart without any finesse. She whimpered and thrust her behind higher. Presumptuous bitch, he thought, tugging her hair cruelly.

Indulging her wasn't a hardship on the odd occasion it suited him. Today, foreplay wasn't going to happen. She wouldn't even murmur in protest, just as she never murmured when he refused to kiss her. Francesca never knew when and what he would decide to do; it kept her eager. He initiated. She followed. He tugged her hair harder. She whimpered again, widening her stance and lifting the smooth tanned skin in a way that made it only too obvious what she wanted, what she always wanted. Her bottom was so tight. Her slit glistened. He pushed her dress up higher. She groaned, and he grinned to himself.

"Do you want my cock here?" he said, thrusting two fingers into her slickness. She moaned but shook her head. He taunted her some more before unzipping his pants. Nico let her go to sheath himself, impatient to be done. He thrust his fingers back inside her and then used the moisture on his fingers around the opening of her anus. Her whole body trembled, and his cock leaped, responding to her excitement. One long finger was replaced by two. She panted, she moaned. She whimpered like a baby. He gave her more. He felt her muscles coiling in anticipation and reached for the little bottle on his desk. Generous with the lubrication didn't mean he gave her warning. Instead he grabbed her hips and thrust deeply. Francesca arched and cried out in pain, the kind of pain she loved.

"Yes, yes. More. Give me more."

"Do you want me to stop?" he asked harshly, his voice roughened by desire. "Answer me."

"God no," she screeched, shoving against him, impatient as always.

"Then don't tell me how I should fuck you." He pulled out and walked around to the front of the desk. She stayed perfectly still under his glare, watching as he moved his hand over his long, hard length. She salivated, licked her lips but remained quiet. He waited, staring and stroking continuously. She didn't make a sound. He walked back behind her and slid into cock heaven. A low groan escaped him at the fit. She was so tight, so desperate to set the pace. Francesca wanted that edgy pleasure badly. Nico smiled to himself. He hadn't intended to get into a serious relationship with her. Surprisingly, they suited each other well.

Francesca's pride or ego kept her faithful. She might like her sex specific and rough, but she wasn't a bed hopper. She felt herself above that. Francesca was a snob whose need to protect her reputation was at odds with her greedy, sexual and often perverse personality. If she wanted to look down on others, he didn't care. He cared that she was fastidious. In public, she used that cultured voice and well-dressed body to advantage. Her intelligence and her ability to act as a hostess were above par. It amused him to know her father was grooming her to take over the family business in the sincere belief his daughter only shit gold nuggets. Francesca ensured her father kept thinking that way. Her sense of superiority wouldn't allow anything less.

The slap of his balls against her flesh was both delicious and painful. It brought him back to the current situation. Nico had work waiting for his attention. He needed to speed things up. Nico reached for her breast, pulling on the piercing so that she bucked against him. She screamed. Her breathing, wild and ragged, egged him on so he allowed it. He relished his control of her orgasms.

Increasing his thrusts to pounding, he used his fingers to mimic his actions in her weeping slit. Nico knew just what she liked. She screamed again, and he let go. *Fuck, it felt good.*

He wasted no time pulling out of her, removed the condom, tied it up and put it into one of the small bags he kept for that purpose. He watched her, noting the smile on her face as she put on her panties. Francesca wasn't at all bothered by the coldness of his withdrawal. It excited her. She saw it as an appetiser for next time. As much as was possible they were happy together in a neat little package. Functioning for him depended on a controlled environment.

He walked to the bathroom and washed his hands, smelling his fingers to ensure no remnant remained of Francesca's essence. He washed them again and looked up in the mirror as he rinsed. *That mouth, that delicious annoying mouth with those full lips that pouted so delightfully at his jibes*, he said to his image in the oval mirror, *was going to get her into so much trouble. She had far too much to say for herself*. He shook himself in annoyance as he realised exactly who he was thinking about. It wasn't Francesca.

Chapter 3

"IS THIS WHAT you bought at the markets? It's just one colour."

"I want it to contrast against the pattern. Can I use the sewing machine again?" Lia never knew if she should say more when Gina instigated these moments of not quite conversation. She had finally decided on keeping replies short and sweet. Gina gave a nod and went back to the letter. This was the letter Papa had sent three months into Mama's remission. Lia knew every word off by heart. *I pray every night that she is really finished with all the pain,* he had written. Her parents had been reconciled at this point, and Lia wasn't sure she could cope if Gina made any cutting comments.

Although lately she had seen a little of the woman she remembered, the thawing process in the cold war between them was slow. Ice was melting though. What surprised Lia was the fact that even if she had begun this process of wanting a truce for her father's sake, she now wanted it for herself. She was so caught up in her musings that she almost missed the moment Gina spoke.

"She suffered a great deal, didn't she?"

Lia nodded and picked up the material in her lap blindly. Her insides ached. Bile rose in her mouth. She forced it down, concentrating fiercely to remain silent and still.

"They loved each other?" This was one of those moments again. Moments Lia wasn't sure she should interrupt by speaking. Gina sounded as if she cared. Her voice was less stilted somehow, less harsh, almost kind.

"Yes," Lia finally whispered. "She told me near the end, that last year of her life was the happiest she had ever been."

"This is difficult for you, isn't it, despite the bravado you insist on whipping me with?" When Angelia didn't reply, her aunt continued. "You know everything, don't you, all the dirty bits and pieces of that awful day?" Gina sighed, a sad sound. "You ask for a lot being here, do you realise that? What is it you want? Because it's not just about these letters, not like in the beginning. And you and Lucio, such an inordinate amount of time spent talking so cosily, what is all that?"

"I like him. I want to bury the past and so does he. I think you know that. I want a family. They, my mother, my father and Lucio, paid a huge price for what they did..."

"And I didn't?"

"Aunt Gina, I know you did. It was terrible, but it's been twenty years. Lucio is still here. I know he's done some stupid things over the years, but you shut him out completely, turned his son against him, and yet he is still here."

"He talks too much."

"Aunt Gina! Please. He doesn't tell me these things. I'm not blind, I see the way things are. My mother paid; the things she faced with her illness you couldn't imagine. Papa paid, he lost her; he lost you. Can this all stop before more people are dead without closure?"

Gina got up and left the room, but not before Lia had seen tears. Bitterness, loss and anger, all three had glided across that pale visage, and yet the real Gina had been there too, the old Gina. Despite the severity of unhappiness etched on that forehead, today something else had broken free. Lia wondered how people could keep feelings so bottled up inside, letting them twist their lives for so long. Her aunt needed time to think. Hell, *she* needed to think. What exactly was she here to accomplish? Gina was right. Much more was involved and all of it painfully frustrating.

"Lia?"

"Uncle Lucio, I didn't hear you come in."

"I didn't want to interrupt. You are so determined, like my son. When you want something, you don't let anything get in the way." Lia winced, and Lucio broke in quickly. "No, I didn't mean that in a bad way. I have watched you; you are kind, gentle, patient and you love her. I can see it. You even tolerate my son while he goes out of his way to make life so difficult." He sighed, weighing his words, understanding she was wary, and rightfully so. "I wanted to tell you…"

"Please don't say you're sorry. I am so sick of sorry. I just want to forget, to move on."

"I know that, but I wanted to, not explain maybe but…" He sighed again. "I know you have details, memories perhaps and it was wrong, what we did. I don't want forgiveness. I do want you to understand."

He stopped talking and she could see he was searching for words. Out of the corner of her eye Lia noted Gina coming back down the hallway. "Uncle Lucio, stop, it doesn't matter." Lia was afraid Lucio might say something to ruin the precarious relationship she and her aunt seemed to be building. Gina's expression and the finger pressed to her aunt's lip silenced her.

"You told Gina we should have closure. You're right. Your mother and I, we never had closure. Closure is important. Gina's pregnancy took priority and so the passion we had for each other wasn't resolved. Now, I know it wouldn't have lasted. Then, your mother and I weren't given the option to find out. It became the ultimate fantasy of *what ifs*. I know it doesn't excuse what Marissa and I did. That summer we met again we were selfish. After living with a fantasy for so long, we couldn't resist finding out if it had a basis. We, your mother and I, selfishly but honestly too, believed we had to find out if it meant something. We were wrong, and in the process of finding out, we destroyed a family." The sound of his sigh was sad, a tiny, pitiful expulsion of breath. "I like it, you, being here. I am so tired of all this drama. I want to turn it off like we do the television. But mostly, I don't want you to hate me."

"God," she said, her voice quivery despite a great effort to maintain neutrality. Lia couldn't dismiss the woman listening, as the man in front of her, bared his soul. "I forced my way into your home and you helped me. I don't hate you. I hate what you did that day. I understand the reasoning if not the deed. Mama explained the same thing to me. We might not be able to forget the past but maybe we can..."

"Maybe we can accept that people can change?"

Longing was there in his face and in his voice. Lia couldn't reply; she didn't know how.

"The trouble is: some us find it harder to believe people can learn from their mistakes. Your mother learned, and your father forgave her. I want the same thing. Convincing Gina and Domenico..."

"You read the letters before they were sent back, didn't you?" Lia wasn't sure where the sudden insight had come from. She only knew it was true.

Lucio blinked, taken back by her perception and the sudden change in conversation. "Yes, I did," he said after a long pause.

"The pain, the honesty...the determination to change things, to make them better broke my heart. I wanted, want...need changes too."

The emotions etched, entrenched in the handsome face broke hers. "I...what...how?" Lia floundered at what to say. She swallowed and waited patiently for him to continue.

"I resealed them very carefully, and then sent them back just as Gina ordered. She doesn't know I read them."

"And so, Uncle, have you? Have you changed?" Lia whispered.

"I think so."

"No more of the women Domenico accuses you of?" Lia watched her aunt put a hand to her mouth. Lucio laughed softly, not at all offended by her words or her manner.

"No. Not for a long, long time actually. You see how I live, so you understand maybe just a little why he thinks it is still going on. But no, despite not sharing a room with my wife except for the odd times she will allow it. I think I grew up finally. I don't think I have to prove anything anymore, so usually it's the bocce, if I am not working or a drink with my friends."

"Why did you stay?" Lia asked, as much for herself as for the woman listening who was wiping tears from her face, just like her husband. His hesitation had her putting the pieces together, so she pushed harder for an answer. "Why did you stay, why are you still here?" For a moment she thought he might not answer. She waited. Both women waited.

"At first because I had no place to go but then...." The silence was deafening.

"You love her!"

"Always," he answered. "It just took me a long time to understand, and I told you despite everything, she cooks, she cleans. She takes very good care of me. I am what you English call *high maintenance,* like your mother. It takes a special person to understand this. That doesn't mean they will forgive easily, my son more so than my wife. And Lia, despite what my son thinks I would give my life for him." He shrugged, looking very lost for a moment and then he picked up his keys and left. Lia watched her aunt back away and knew this little episode was not up for discussion.

The planned visit to see Ashlee and Greg for the weekend was a godsend. Time apart could be a good thing. Lia needed to get her head around this and was grateful that she had friends of her own. A miracle, the couple were her own little miracle in this sea of emotion. Things were moving quickly and in a direction that was too exciting to miss. Lia had been the catalyst, it would appear, for much more than anyone could have bargained for. Lucio might get his wife back, Papa would get his sister back, and if he wasn't here to enjoy it, Lia was.

Lia sat at the table, her hand moving lovingly over the shiny surface, and considered the repercussions of remaining longer. Laura would not be happy, but she would accept it. Domenico would be a problem. Lia quivered involuntarily as she pictured the hard lines of his face. At times he reminded her of the military heroes featured on the covers of romance books. Short, cropped hair in severe, motionless faces, the men defied logic and managed to look unearthly beautiful despite the weapons strapped to their bodies. How would he react if things happened between his parents, and why was it, she wondered, any thoughts concerning him always sent her heart into overdrive?

Chapter 4

"GREG JUST called. He's organised the job interview at the base for today." Lia could not believe her luck. A job at the American army base, Sigonella, would make life so much more interesting. She loved Sicily, but she needed to be doing more if she continued to stay here.

"So, is this babbling you're doing supposed to interest me in any way?" Domenico asked from the recliner on the balcony.

"I need to be there quickly, so I can talk to him first, and I thought you might drive me. Please." She had no illusions about him, but she could hope, and maybe her excitement was contagious. Lia had been living here in her family's home for just over four months. Domenico however still barely tolerated her presence, even if he was a little more civil in front of his parents than times like these, where only the two of them were present.

"Please," she asked, not above begging. He just didn't understand how much she loved it here, how at home she felt surrounded by family. He disapproved vehemently that Lia had won over his mother.

"I'm busy. You get the bus from here on the days you go stay with your friends."

"It will be so much easier if you drive me, please, just this one time? Domenico? Please?"

"I'm busy." Lia bit her lip at the blatant lie. He was reading the paper. He looked up, and as always, she had to fight to not react under his piercing scrutiny. Something in his directness, the way he blatantly took in her body, what she wore and how she moved, rattled her peace of mind. At some level she accepted their bickering was safe, but right now it was all she could do not to hit him.

She blew out a breath. He had been more difficult of late, sensing the change in the atmosphere at home between his parents. Domenico hated feeling out of the loop. He didn't understand what was happening. To him it made no sense. His father had done the unforgivable and no white flag could ever be waved. He blamed Lia for the atmosphere he couldn't quite get a handle on. Lia never knew how she got inside his head, but she did. Asking him to help her had been foolish. She had just fed him ammunition for his frustrations. Yet last night he had brought home some of the sweets his mother loved and had included some for Lia. This morning he was a jerk again. Lia huffed. He smirked. Lia knew as she always did with him, that backing off achieved more, until the next round.

"Fine! I'll get the bus." She turned away and raced back to her room. If she missed this bus it would be another hour. Five minutes later she was out the door, with the sound of Domenico's laughter dogging her footsteps.

"Bus is pretty close to the stop," she heard Domenico yell, and bit back a retort.

His position gave him an excellent view of the main street and giving him the finger from downstairs would be childish. Lia knew it amused him that she wasn't above being vulgar, at least where he was concerned. Lia tugged at her hair, thinking her campaign to win back her childhood hero might have to be put to rest, buried at least six feet under.

She was perversely reluctant to let the idea go completely. In the dark recesses of her mind again, something niggled and questioned her reluctance to look further. In this moment however when he was behaving like a complete arse, Lia wondered why she bothered to analyse things. Fuck him, she thought, as the lift sounded her arrival on the ground floor. She raced out of the apartment block.

Upstairs Domenico stood to watch her. Part of him felt bad at having refused to help her. It didn't last long. He didn't want her here. All that sweetness and light was sickening. He didn't believe the act for a second. She was Marissa's daughter, evidenced by the way she had his father wrapped around her finger. He wasn't blind to the way his friends looked at her, even Marco. *Brainless idiots swayed by a body*... He stopped himself at that point, annoyed, because thinking about her body, or the way the bathroom smelled after she had used it, a scent so essentially Lia lingering in his memory hours afterwards, made him... He slowly unclenched his fists and deliberately changed the course of his thoughts. She was clever. She never left a thing out of place in there or in the study they shared.

Domenico considered everything she did as premeditated, calculated. It had to be. She ensured things were put back exactly the way he liked. Why did she not take the opportunity to annoy him? Lia confused him. She was so fucking perfect. Even her teeth were perfect, small and even and white although the mouth enclosing them could even make him blush when he got her started. Not that his mother ever saw that side, no matter how hard he pushed it to happen. Had his mother seriously forgotten this irritating little brat had forced her way into their lives? And what the fuck was happening with Gina and the old man now?

Domenico felt it the moment Lia looked up. Even from the distance of four floors up, their eyes met and held. She was furious. He laughed when that finger went up. She turned away as her attention was caught by the bus gliding closer. He watched as she saw her chance and darted across the road. *Stupid girl!* He knew straight away she had forgotten they drove on the opposite side of the road. He grinned, enjoying her desperation. The humour quickly disappeared when Domenico realised she hadn't seen the yellow Vespa.

"Fuck," he mouthed in English, along with other things in Italian, as the Vespa hit her. "God, damn you Lia!" Still cursing, he raced downstairs, not waiting for the lift.

There was a throng of people around her and a very apologetic rider. Like some waif Lia sat on the ground, assuring the old gentleman she was fine and that it hadn't been his fault. Her legs were grazed, and her stockings torn. Her hair was not doing a good job hiding a nasty wound on her forehead, yet she was only concerned with calming the rider in that infuriatingly soft, sweet voice. He pushed past a few people standing around her and bent down in front of her, not sure of his reception, but unable to stop himself. He was partly to blame for this and the sooner he sorted it out the better.

"Oh Domenico, I missed the bus," she wailed, and then did the unexpected: held up her arms towards him.

He had an odd feeling in his chest as he bent to pick her up. He shrugged it away, just like the thought that she fitted perfectly in his arms. Carrying her back inside the building, he concentrated on trying to ignore how much he loathed the smell and look of blood. A weakness, one he couldn't control, and she was making a mess of him and his clothes with hers. This was so typical of Lia, Domenico thought, taking refuge in irritation and gritting his teeth. He couldn't enjoy a day away from work.

Unfortunately, his sense of honour wouldn't let him deny he had deliberately goaded her into being careless. She seemed small and fragile as he carried her; it triggered a faint memory. *Jesus! Trust her to turn his peaceful life into a fucking soap opera.* Something about the way she had held up her arms continued to nag at him. He opened the door, took her inside where he dumped her on the couch. She whimpered. Domenico scowled and walked to the linen press.

Grabbing the first aid kit and some towels Domenico donned surgical gloves before touching her again. Most of the injuries were on the surface, but he grimaced anyway and wondered whether she needed a doctor. All that blood was making him queasy and his face must have reflected this because she was quiet. At least she wasn't crying anymore. For some reason the tears had made him most uncomfortable. After the initial wail, the tears had petered out.

She had grazes on both legs, a deep cut of some kind on her wrist and a scratch across the side of her face just above her eye. He was worried about the dirt she had picked up off the road. After patching her up as best he could, he washed her face and wiped her legs, pulling down the ruined stockings to facilitate the process. She wore stay ups. He scowled once again as he moved the cloth up the tanned leg.

It's okay," she said suddenly, her face flushing with colour as she stared at his hand on the top of her thigh. "I should have been looking. I can finish this. Really, it's fine. But could you bring me the phone, so I can ring Greg please?"

Domenico ignored her as if she hadn't spoken, and continued the wiping movement, pushing aside the flowing fabric of her skirt and catching a glimpse of pink lace. As if sensing what he could see, Lia fiddled with the blue material, re-covering the soft smooth skin out of his sight. He continued cleaning. *Pale pink high cut lace, probably with the matching bra*, he thought and barely preventing another scowl.

Sharing space in his home meant there was very little he didn't know about her. The washing drying on the balcony, told its own tale. She had good pieces: lacy, more sensual than sexy, mixed with plain, tasteful and comfortable pieces. No thongs, which he found fascinating for some perverse reason. Fuck, he couldn't believe his errant thoughts. She was a distraction. He moved away from her. His abrupt, angry movement caused her to recoil.

"I'll ring Marco," he said, trying to sound less irritated with her at the expression on her face. The cut at her wrist looked nasty. He followed the movement as she worked her top teeth over her bottom lip.

"No! It's not necessary. I'm fine, and in any case, Greg will know what do. He's a doctor too and I don't want to ruin the chance for this job." At his narrowed eyes, she added quietly, "please, just get me the phone?"

Domenico grabbed the handset and threw it at the sofa, so it landed beside her. She smiled her thanks and dialled. He hated her quiet dignity. It made him feel like the villain. At a profound level he knew she was genuine. *Why couldn't he just accept that and her?* He sat down beside her, glad to see the graze at her forehead had stopped bleeding.

"Thank you," she said after a brief conversation, putting her hand on his arm and handing him back the phone with her other hand. He stared at the spot where her hand and his arm met. "Greg is coming here and taking me back to the base for a few days." She quickly removed her hand.

He was relieved but not sure why. Was it the fact she had moved her hand, or that Greg picking her up meant his parents could be left out of this incident? Why did this bright, intelligent, and beautiful creature put him more on edge than any sharp knife?

"Good, in fact why don't you consider making that your home instead, or better still going home to Australia? My mother has read the damned letters; you've achieved your purpose so why are you trying to get a job?" His abruptness hurt her. This time she cringed. He didn't care. He couldn't help himself. Correction, he didn't want to help himself. Knowing he wanted her gone was enough for him. He felt the tick at the side of his mouth as she held his gaze. For a moment Nico was caught in the spell of a moment he didn't understand. He would have sworn she too felt it too. It flashed for an instance between them and was gone.

"And the arsehole is back." she murmured, standing up shakily. She ignored the hand he offered and limped to her room. "Fuck you!" she added for good measure, loud enough to ensure he heard.

He grinned at the language, relieved to be back in the relationship he understood. He refrained from answering. She amused him. She amused him a little too much for comfort. It got his ire up again.

"Did you forget you told your friend Laura that the arsehole looks like a Greek God just yesterday, on Skype no less?"

"With worse manners than a baboon was what I followed up with, or did you forget that part because you were too busy swaggering out in just a towel? That was pathetic even for you!"

"It didn't stop you or your friend from looking, did it? Were you hoping the towel wouldn't hold?"

"Please, of course we were. With the things I have told Laura, your arrogance being top of the list, we were hoping to see how small a dick you had. You must be compensating for something, to be so full of yourself."

"I'll get you a tape measure and let you see for yourself, although it's a little disturbing to know you have a need to discuss my anatomy."

"Do you hear yourself? Do you know how childish your behaviour is? Why would you walk out in a towel?"

"Why, you want to know why? This is my home, mine not yours. If you weren't here what I wore wouldn't matter, would it? Maybe you should take the hint? Neither I, or my anatomy wants you here."

She held her tongue and limped to her room, slamming her door as an answer to his taunts. His laugh echoed as she got herself ready. Sometimes she hated him so much she was afraid.

Unexpected Passion (an extract)

The Unexpected Series Book 2

THE UNEXPECTED SERIES/BOOK **2**

Book 2, Unexpected Passion will centre on Alexia and Ricardo. These two strong-willed characters have more in common with each other than either one would suspect. Secrets will be revealed, and passions will surprise them both.

Alexia (Lexi to her friends and family), the heroine of the second book has a Greek background and is Lia's Godmother. Lia is the female lead in the first book of the series, Unexpected Obsession. Although I have designed the series so that each book stands alone the books do link. I wanted the people in my novels to be a family of sorts, and because in Australia we are very much multi-cultural country, I also wanted my characters to reflect this.

Lia organises a trip for Alexia that covers Italy, Greece and Turkey. Without giving spoilers our Lexi will spend time with Lia whilst in Italy. We don't exist in isolation and I thought it nice if we could continue learning more about Lia and Nico as the years progressed. This will weave through Alexia's and Ricardo romance but make no mistake this is most definitely their love story. Please read on.

Author's note: This is still very much a raw extract and will need editing. I hope you like this enough to come back for more when I publish it early in 2019. Feel free to give me feedback on this at my email address above.

Chapter 1

Alexia Georgiou was annoyed. Too many people had time on their hands and were using it to interfere in her life. Take her friend Fran, her supposedly best friend, had just spent a full two hours lecturing Alexia on packing, the packing for her trip, not Fran's trip, but hers. Fran didn't have a bee in her bonnet, she had wasps that flapped around criticising every item Alexia had put in her suitcase. The cow had pulled everything out, tossing them all over the room. *Seriously*, Alexia thought to herself, *it was her holiday and she wanted to be comfortable. Screw Fran, screw her niece Julie and screw just about everyone else she knew.*

Lexi walked past the mirror in her lounge room, determined to ignore the hair comment as well. She got three steps past it before she stopped and turned around. It needed a cut again, and yes, she conceded to her alter ego's smug reflection, with a scowl, a colour wouldn't go astray either. *Damn it. Why won't they let me lead my own life? Why does everyone assume I need fixing? If they had kept their traps shut, I wouldn't be double guessing myself.* The person in the mirror had bags under her eyes and was carrying about six kilos more than needed, so didn't answer. *Oh! Shut up! Ten kilos, then! Are you happy now?* Alexia scowled at the reflection, furious that she couldn't lie to herself. She had a week before she took off, so a hair appointment doable if she organised herself. It might be the easy compromise to keep the busy bodies happy.

She blew out a frustrated breath because Fran had made some sense. "Fran might have had a *bit of right* on her side about the hair. The bitch!" Lexi spoke the words with a British accent and a snooty look on her face. The mirror didn't laugh. *A picture did speak a thousand words.* Lexi puffed out a whoosh of air, watching it land on the mirror as mist. Leaning in, she wiped the glass and stared at the steel grey wisps, a harsh halo against her complexion; the bits of faded colour in some of the strands long past renewable. The grey washed out the pale blue of her eyes completely, and her eyes fringed by dark lashes were her best feature. Alexia had gone grey at nineteen years of age. There had been no explanation; overnight the muddy strands of brown had acquired a greyish tinge, and the change continued until the grey dominated.

To counteract the effect sensibly, Alexia had decided on streaks. The strands of gold and reddish copper had become a trade mark, surprisingly easy to maintain, and adding a distinctive look that complemented her barely five-foot height and athletic build. Alexia had made her big breasts, small waist and nicely rounded behind work for her and had never lacked male attention, at least not till the last couple of years.

The face in the mirror had too much to say. Alexia poked her tongue at her reflection and picked up the phone. Idly she brushed her hands over the dark mahogany bookcase that sat underneath the oval mirror. Dust, she scowled again and wiped her hands on her pants. Maybe it was time she made some changes, beginning with herself. *Oh, the irony of it all!* She needed to change back to what she had been rather than change to something new.

Fuck! How did I let my nails get to this stage? It's not like I was busy dusting. She was in a rut, the worst kind – the kind where she didn't feel like doing anything. She dialled Trish's number. The woman would scream with glee, to get her hands back on Alexia's head for more than a trim. It would be like the scene from Moonstruck where Cher finally agrees to cover the grey.

Lexi hated the well-meaning conspiracy between her friends. She knew it meant she was an unappreciative bitch. She didn't care. They pissed her off because they were right. She dialled her hairdresser's number between curses. *I wonder if Trish has time to organise my nails.* Her reflection scrunched itself into a sneer. For the first time in a long time Alexia ignored her own negativity and let herself laugh. She had to; she looked like a damned maniac.

***

Two days later and halfway around the world, Lia put down the phone, smiling. Fran had come through with the measurements she needed to complete her little project. How Fran had managed to get Alexia to agree to having her wobbly bits measured, testified to Fran's determination, proof of how much Fran cared about her friend. She had concocted some story about a party Lia and Nico were hosting during the month Alexia would stay with them in Sicily, and that Lia wanted to make her a dress as a birthday present.

A plausible enough tale, Lia thought, given Lexi had decided to extend her visit and celebrate not only her own birthday, but also the possible birth of Lia's new baby before heading home. Lia smirked on two levels; Lexi would have some unexpected additions to her wardrobe and Lia and Nico would partake in a feast of delicious Greek food. Alexia Georgiou didn't cook, she created magic.

Lexi's slump into depression after her mother's death had frightened all those who loved Lexi. Although looking after Yiayia had drained her, Lexi had idolised the woman and the loss had devastated her. Yiayia, the Greek word for grandmother and a word Lia had used since a small child, had been a loveable blend of sweetness and roguishness. The dear old thing determined early on that if Lia didn't have a grandmother of her own, she would fill that role. Yiayia, with her short-bread biscuits, had filled that role for many if truth be told including Lia's best friend Laura.

That death had come a year after the death of Lia's Papa. He and Lexi had been best friends for nearly thirty years, and Lia suspected he would have been the one to best help Lexi through the trauma. From a teenager, Lia had secretly hoped Lexi, already a mother figure, would become a more permanent part of their lives. Instead the friendship held. There were time times Lia had wondered if they had all missed something, some clue. It had never made sense to her that two people so in tune had not become more.

Lia snapped back to the present, recalling the conversation, she'd just had with Fran. Lia hated being so far away from her friends even if living in Sicily agreed with her.
Fortunately, Nico was open to visiting Sydney at any stage after the baby was born. For now, the trip meant Lexi would be here soon and Lia could smother her in as much love as Lexi would allow. Smoothing the indigo fabric and calculating how much trim she would have to buy, the sound of the

door opening startled her. She tightened the belt on the jade silk dressing gown and walked out of the study.

Her heart fluttered. Moisture pooled in that special place despite the clumsiness of the huge bump on the front of her body. Or maybe it was because of the bump? *Didn't pregnancy make you too tired for sex?* Then again, not many pregnant women had a husband like hers. Lia willed her face into a bland expression. *Too late*, she thought. His beautifully cut black trousers were tenting. She raised her brows at her husband. He laughed and kept walking the direct line to where she now stood.

"I've just had my shower. Stay away." He laughed again. *Damn the man in front of her.* She held that thought and a pout for at least five seconds. He lifted her onto the breakfast bar. He had a fetish about its height, calling it perfect for his use. Lots of furniture pieces in their home were perfect, according to Nico. "Why are you home so early? Our lunch date isn't for another couple of hours."

Nico's senses came alive at her fragrance. Arousal happened just by looking at her but when combined with coconut, cinnamon and chocolate it was impossible to reason with his cock. "My client cancelled, and I thought to myself, what can I do with the spare time? I can do some paperwork, or I could go home and spend quality time with my wife, especially when my Mamma is looking after our son."

"Damn it, you're going to mess me up, aren't you?"

"Well, if it's too much trouble I could read a book instead."

"What has reading a book got to do with the hands untying my robe…" Lia stopped talking when one of those beautifully shaped hands pushed her gently onto her back while the other wandered over the prominent belly. He bent and kissed his child before letting his lips follow a determined path.

"Nico." She whimpered as his tongue reached its target and licked the length of it.

"Do you want me to stop?"

She shook her head, too breathless to speak, and closed her eyes. The wicked instrument not only licked again but darted inside. He was slow, leisurely letting his mouth show her where his head had been all morning. She moaned, fighting the need to watch knowing it gave him a heady sense of power. Her lashes though had a mind of their own, lifting to enjoy the view, knowing full well any objections would be token.

Nico's raised brows confirmed he had been waiting for the eye contact. He grinned while his tongue continued it path to dissolve her insides. His actions were secondary. The evil man knew her well. Using her arms as leverage she raised herself onto her elbows. One hand wrapped itself in his soft dark hair. She dug her nails hard into his scalp knowing how much he relished it, his soft growls vibrating against her delicate skin. Her hormones were in permanent overdrive. His? God knew the answer to that one.

Lia tugged his hair to lift his face to hers. She barely touched his lips before he took over. He made her desperate at the best of times, but the taste of herself on his tongue scrambled her mind completely. Aggressively she thrust her tongue against his, letting him know she was ready for whatever he wanted.

Nico in turn wondered whether he would ever get enough of this woman who looked like an angel and turned into a flow of lava at his touch. He kissed her ferociously, letting the tongue that had been lapping at her essence mix with the clean fresh taste she offered. At that moment a part of him wanted her mouth on him, wanted to push his way in and fuck her mouth till he came. He craved that combined essence like a man starved for air. His impatient headstrong cock had other ideas. He kicked his pants away and let his hard length fill her.

It never failed to surprise her, this intense pleasure she received just having him inside of her. Their tongues continued to battle, mimicking the dance of body parts, pulsing and throbbing until her insides tightened, her slick softness demanding the steel rod melt against her. She moaned into his mouth as she fragmented, pushing him into his release. Sated he slumped over her, his head on her breast.

"You know," he said, his tone casual, his lips moving over her still covered nipple and breaking the quiet. "I can't decide what the man in the apartment opposite finds the most entertaining, you in this position or me without my pants."

"What? That's not possible." She cried. He grinned, and she punched at his chest, mouthing an obscenity in response to his teasing.
"What a terrible mouth you have at times. Just as well you can make better use of it at other times! You do realise he is too far across the way to see us."

"Would it bother you if he could see us?" The look he gave her made her smile. "You are a crazy perverted man. "

"You have to admit, there's a lot worthwhile to see."

His tone sent those little shivers back into play. She watched as he slid out of her and used the dressing gown to wipe himself, and then do the same for her. She punched him again for good measure.

"Lia," he asked, suddenly losing the humour in his face and moving one hand to her throat. He applied the smallest amount of pressure.

She waited quietly. When he did that it was because he felt overwhelmed. Since he had accepted she was having this second child, he had moments when he needed to exert control. He felt he had power over her this way, or so he thought. Lia let him believe it. Some people might not understand. They had no idea of how his mind worked. Lia did. His thumb made small circles at the base of throat. Still he said nothing. He took a breath, taking her hand with his, he used the thumb of that hand to rub lightly over her engagement ring. She wondered if he knew that his left thumb was imitating his right one.

"How did you know this was the ring I wanted you to choose?"
Careful not to react to the strange way his mind worked, she let out a small sigh at the question almost three years overdue. That meant three years of thinking about it, three long years. She smiled gently and turned to him as if he had asked a perfectly simple question. "Nico, it was a square ruby, with two small square diamonds. The symmetry was perfect, the stones were bold, and the ring combined yellow and white gold. It suited us both. Of course, it would be the one you wanted. It was perfect." She crinkled her nose at him. "I imagine Seppo would have received some very exact instructions. And, I'm not surprised he could fill them. His store was full of things that would appeal. You're his landlord, aren't you?" She raised a brow and he flushed slightly. She lifted her fingers to his

cheek and he leaned in, letting her soothe him. "Nico, I know who you are."

"Yes, you do. Why?"

She didn't answer, knowing full well he wasn't ready yet. His silence indicated his own awareness of the fact. His hand continued the small caress at her throat before lifting her off the table, his face re-arranging itself to the relaxed man who had come home early just to make love to her. She bent down to pick up his things.

"Don't. Leave them," he whispered against her ear. He inhaled her fragrance as she tightened her arms around his neck and put her cheek against his. He liked that he didn't have to explain himself.

"Did you sort out Alexia?"

"Yes, I did. I have some bits and pieces to finish she doesn't know. Hopefully I can finish in time for you to deliver when you fly to Rome, although I'm pretty confident I can."

"Good." He kissed her as swung her into his arms carry her to their bedroom. "No reason then not to concentrate on your husband."

Chapter 2

"*Where was the sign?*" There was supposed to be, a sign somewhere and Alexia Georgiou refused to take her medication in response to the agitation knocking at her mind. Anxiety had been her enemy too long. She would not panic. *She could speak the language and she was a mature person, fifty-four years old, and surely this counted for something? That's damn right. I won't panic.* She stopped to look around her reminding herself to breathe, to stay calm. Lia's friend Annalisa had seemed very efficient in all their conversations, she reassured herself.

The airport, big, noisy and so busy disconcerted her after the smoothness of the trip. *I've got to get a grip on myself, stop this infernal shaking and I'll be fine. Oh God, I've also got to stop talking to myself out loud. Shit, starting now.* She ignored the look the woman gave her but then found herself relenting. The woman recognised a case of nerves and the look appeared genuinely sympathetic. Lexi gave a small shy smile. The smile she received in return bolstered her along with the woman's words. "Tutto á posto?"

"Si, grazie." A stranger asking her if all was well settled her nerves. Lexi turned with more determination. After all she had been to Italy before even if that had been a different time with less people crowding around. She had succumbed to superstition many years ago and thrown a coin into the Trevi Fountain, several coins, and they had brought her back. Maybe magic existed. Lord knew she could use some.

That was the real problem, not the crowed Rome airport, but the realisation that somewhere along the line over the last few years she had run out of the energy to believe in anything. The smallest things unnerved her, overwhelmed her including this trip. Acknowledging it as a good idea, didn't make it easier to be here. She wished it did because she certainly needed to relax and enjoy life again. She needed to push the panic down and keep it from ruining every experience. Breathing deep she reminded herself that travel meant adventure, a chance to find the *fun Lexi* again.

"Signorina Georgiou?" The voice, rich in tone in the way of Italian men, had a delicious accent giving her Greek name a European class which Alexia relished. Maybe her determination to embrace good vibes would pay off. She felt tingly at the timbre of his greeting. Turning to face the voice, that view was quickly challenged. The man in front of her crushed all positive thoughts and brought Negative Nellie back to the surface.

The man had yellow-brown eyes in a tanned face, cat's eyes. *Did that make sense? Did people have yellow eyes?* He frowned. *Oh shit, did I say that aloud? Too bad!* Lexi continued her slow perusal. The man remained silent. Long dark, dirty-dark blonde hair tied back in a pony tail, greeted Lexi along with an earring in his left ear and an almighty sleeve of a tattoo, or did people call it a tattoo sleeve she wondered? It started at the wrist and climbed its way past the biceps on his right arm. The thing looked like a rose bush, a climbing rose decked in glorious pinks against a green-leafed backdrop.

Lexi had to admit, it had a certain charm, could be termed beautiful not that she liked tattoos, well maybe smaller ones. Surprisingly the bevy of roses added to the aura of alpha masculinity. Those tiger eyes made sure of that. He was wearing a white T-shirt, spoiled in her opinion, by the evil glare of the black skull emblazed across the chest area. She couldn't help it. Her nose wrinkled, her lips pursed unpleasantly as she continued her perusal. The man had on very well-fitting blue jeans totally ruined by the rip on one thigh and the several smaller rips on the knee and calf of the other leg. Unfortunately for her he was also wearing a badge that identified him as Ricardo from 'Paradiso Tours".

"Fuck! You have to be kidding me!" Alexia whispered, under her breath. *It was supposed to be under her breath but judging from his reaction it may have been a teeny bit louder than that.* The polite interest he had been displaying inched up a notch. There was a sudden gleam in the golden eyes that she couldn't quite read but she knew enough to know it didn't reflect well on her. The tilt of his head announced only too well that he meant it as a superior look. Now he was the one perusing her outfit, her, Flattering was not in the vocabulary of his piercing eyes.

Ricardo, she knew instinctively, was thinking the old bag had a few problems with the way she saw the world. His eyes, expressive and narrowed, branded her as one of those people that judged the surface instead of the person underneath. She felt it and he couldn't be faulted for it. She did, him at least. Normally a pragmatic person, Lexi accepted rather than judged. The last few years tolerance had taken a beating but her reading of people had remained.

Lexi swore she could see and feel his mind working to put the thoughts together. Lexi had spent too many years in a classroom with too many varying personalities not too recognise *the look*. The conversation in his brain went like this - of course he had to be the odd one, not her in her regulation navy track pants, matching zippered jacket and tourist running shoes. Lexi could feel the distain. Hell, she could practically taste it and for once Alexia wished with all her heart she wasn't so good at reading people.
Her honesty screamed the fault as her own.

Defensive, she had judged him. He had reacted accordingly. *Why the hell did she care, what he might be thinking anyway*? Pulling herself together and settling her features into a neutrally pleasant expression, an oxymoron she knew, Lexi offered him her hand. The grip was strong and surprisingly warm. To his credit he recognised that she had had read him and he rearranged his features into a friendlier, more welcoming look but the gleam in his eyes remained. He found her amusing.

Of course, this could also be just a conversation in her head and he might not be thinking anything. No, Alexia knew better. This man had hidden layers despite the hippie look. *Did people still say hippie, or did 'out there' fit better?* Either way, he was too old to dress like that. *Was he even a real Italian? Weren't they all well-dressed, smooth and charming by nationality?* She dug deep into her memories of her first time in their country and she was positive it had been different.

This guy looked like he should be on a surfboard at the beach or in a rock band, not representing some fancy tour company. *To be fair, his age negated the rock band notion even if things these days were more relaxed. He had to be in his fifties. Well, that didn't bode too well, did it? Damn!* Lexi did not find the idea of being stuck on a six-week tour with a 'wanabee-young', middle-aged flower-child instead of a professional. She'd bet a lot of money on the fact that bimbos were his favourite hobby. *What the hell?*

Ricardo was trying not to let his feelings show. His amusement lessened the more those lips of hers disappeared into that fake almost-smile. This was so typical of this generation of female no matter where they came from, always so ready to judge on appearance as if she could talk. *Pazienza, Ricardo*, he told himself as he repeated his question to her again. He needed an acknowledgement about her bags. Maybe he should let her have her fill of looking, at his arm, his hair, his earing and yes, the arm again. *Ma dai, ancora con questo sguardo? Get over yourself lady!* Pointedly he looked down at her luggage and back up at her face hoping to snap her attention back to his question. "Is this all you have?"

"Yes. Yes, it is." She hated sounding rattled. His fixed gaze though unnerved her. She felt measured and found wanting. Mind you, who didn't these days? Ridiculous to start her trip in this manner, with this man she barely knew. There she went again, feeling sorry for herself. Hadn't she just made up her mind to relax?

"Good. Follow me please," he said firmly, making sure he had her attention, and kept it.

She nodded, feeling a little silly, as he grabbed the blue suitcase. He led her back to the small transit vehicle. She saw three possible couples and two elderly ladies all chatting excitedly together. "Fuck! They're all American! Geez Fran, you should have come with me. This is a nightmare," she exclaimed hearing their accented voices and bit her lip as Ricardo glanced back at her. She needed a filter big time for her mouth, or at least she needed to concentrate on thinking things in her head and not saying them out loud. But come on, nearly all the people she knew that had taken tours in Europe, had warned her about loud whining Americans, so she could be forgiven for reacting the way she did.

He, Ricardo obviously disagreed, and thought her the problem. *Shit, she was the problem. Hadn't she gone off her head at the very people who had said that? Great. She was being a real cow, a judgemental bitch. Yellow eyes thought so, and she couldn't blame him. What the hell was wrong with her?* She had agreed to all of this. Ricardo, of Paradiso Tours, had every right to raise those brows, and give her that look.

The chatting had stopped. Curious and friendly smiles came her way as she boarded. She surmised the only one to have heard her little outburst was the blonde bozo. *Lucky for me!* Lexi winced, feeling awkward enough without her mouth antagonizing people before the tour even started. She smiled back and sat down quietly fiddling with her small backpack. She didn't know whether she could do this. She wasn't ready for all these people. Alexia didn't know what was worse, her fear or the battle to keep it hidden. The golden hues had darkened to a deep brown and were staring at her in the rear-view mirror. She cringed further inside her head. Her shoulders followed suit as she realised he didn't like her and wasn't hiding it behind a polite mask. It wasn't good business but at least he was honest.

The Narrow Hallway (an extract)

Author's note: This extract is also very much a raw extract and will also need editing. I hope you like this enough to come back for more. I hope to be able to publish early 2019. Feel free to give me feedback on this at my email address above.

Prologue

The Speaker, a tall man, dominated the room. Resplendent in white, the colour a symbol of purity, the cloak floated around him, gleaming with a life of its own. Heavy silk and lined internally with a fabric simulating animal-fur, the formal apparel donned by all present, gave a sense of unity. Despite covered heads shrouding the faces of the stilled robotic-like forms, they were one as they awaited the final word.

"It is decided, then? Agreed?"

The Others nodded, fearful of, but satisfied with,

the outcome. Sorrow, attached every time this situation arose, kept them silent. Each time an individual became a Watcher and received their instructions, apprehension ruled. The world continued its uneven weave, and the decision to spare the suffering for The Chosen became more emotional and difficult. Both Watcher and Chosen would bind, would share an exclusive synchronicity without a foreseen outcome.

Bodies, individuality hooded and hidden in the sacred robes, bowed their heads in prayer together with The Speaker. A frozen mural, waiting patiently as the heavy fury of steps dissipated, and as the newly-made Watcher left them behind, they did not flinch as he slammed the door. His anger did not rob them of hope. They had after all expected it.

Part One

The Now

The Watcher

"Will you be back soon?"

"I don't know. There's less light these days. Winter's being a real shit. You know I need the light to return. The freaking hallway is playing stupid mind games. Dark and so drab. I hate it."

"I'll miss you. I hate it here alone."

My eyes, I swear, rolled back in my head of their own volition. I couldn't control it. *For fucks sake I was going to work, not the moon! This whining had to stop!* The urge to shake her and yell abuse at her, clogged my throat. Clearing it, I turned to her and gentled my voice. "I might have to stay longer, you know I don't have a choice. I need light to re-coup my energy. I'll be back when I'm back." We went through this every time I received the call these days, and patience was a battle, my own personal anger management arena. Pulling on reserves I waited for her to say more. She always said more.

"Please don't be annoyed. Something is different, worse somehow, and I am so afraid you won't come back. What will happen to me?"

"For fuck's sake, get over this. Nothing will happen to you. Stay inside. I will come back. Don't I always come back?"

Biting viciously on her bottom lip, a nervous habit that no longer excited me, her voice lowered, softened as she spoke until I could barely hear her, not that I needed the words. They never altered.

"I can't help it. I'm afraid."

God, she had become so annoying, clinging in a way I found cloying and oppressive. A part of me felt bad. I shouldn't be so impatient, shouldn't let her get to me. A body length away, I felt her tremor as she reached for me, and wondered with a calmer part of my mind, whether the fault belonged to her crazy fears, justified, given the continued changes in the hallway, and how much could be attributed to her absurd conviction I no longer cared for her. Everything these days spelled rejection.

What was she dreaming up in that broken brain? A drop of blood fell, her top lip a victim to the clean, white teeth. Perfect teeth, perfect like all her features: the small nose, the almond-shaped brown eyes, the impossibly long lashes tracing the smooth skin of the high cheek-bones. The blood continued to pool and fall as she bit harder, a bizarre sensuality as it slid to the side of her mouth in perfect pearl shapes on perfect, too pale, porcelain. When had she become so colourless, so thin, and so brittle? Last night as I fucked her, my hands had caressed hip bones, a dissolving body shape.

"Watcher, please, please don't be angry. Tonight has ...is...feels...I don't know but the fear is choking me. I can't breathe. I hate her. Every time you come back a part of you is gone. She's bad for you, a vampire sucking your life force. You wouldn't need the light so much if she didn't treat you the way she does. It's getting worse and there's not enough of you left, to survive it, to survive her. "

"Stop. Stop right now. This jealousy is absurd. Your paranoia is doing my fucking head in."

"Watcher, are you angry... are you really angry with me? Or with her because you know I'm right? Something is not right, she has to go, she..."

One hand closed over the luscious mouth. I wiped the blood sitting at the corner of her lips away with my thumb as my other hand circled her throat, tightening, gripping hard enough to leave angry red marks. I sighed. My mind a war zone, anger tinged the patience I needed with this fragile being, tinged then opened its mouth, swallowed and regurgitated fury. I knew her words shrieked a truth, I knew Bella had the right to say it; after all she wore the results every time I came home, suffered the violence I brought with me, shared the toll it took on me, felt the repercussions in the harsh, cruel way I took her.

Perhaps if she was different I would be different, things would be different, wouldn't they? When had this virulent hatred of my charge taken her over? Obsession had me hear the same thing over and over until my head was ready to split apart. Just once couldn't Bella take responsibility for herself? Maybe if she wasn't so weak...so whiny I would handle my side of things, especially my job better? Where was the woman I met that night, the woman with so much life, an independent, sensual goddess?

Goddess, not an exaggeration. I remember thinking fortunate had finally smiled on me, and big time. I had some crazy idea she was my bonus for all the shit I had to put up with. What can I say? The girl was a stunner, not young but with the kind of beauty that transcends age, transcends everything. The club that night had been crowded, more so than usual but for me she had stood out like a, I don't know, a beacon. I know that sounds clichéd. I didn't have the words then for her and not now even with all this shit going on, driving both of us into an asylum and not the good or safe kind. I just knew if it was the last thing I did that night I would meet her, talk to her face-to-face, and I would be the one taking her home.

She had noticed me. I could tell despite the way she ducked her head behind that cloud of curly hair that framed her face. For all her beauty she wore an air of shyness indicating uncertainty. I liked that. I liked that someone so beautiful lacked confidence. It meant she took nothing for granted. A protective streak, normally reserved for my charge, took over, softened my stance. Her lips trembled but she smiled, she fucking smiled.

"Nice tattoo," I had said smoothly, letting my fingers glide gently over the small butterfly on her shoulder. Truly it was a work of art, a black, pink and vibrant blue flutter of wings sitting on a delicate branch with tiny green leaves. I had worked my way around the room until her left shoulder, bare and with a soft golden glow enticing me, sat a small breath of distance from my lips. "Got any more?" I whispered, as my lips slid to her ear. I blew on the tiny gold stud and she shivered, blushed, and leaned closer with a sweetness, a gentleness, and delicacy, a juxtaposition to the sultry looks. My heart and cock shook hands, united in their goal to have her.

"Maybe, maybe not."

My cock twitched again, pushed against the prison bars of my zipper, as she answered my question. "Bella," I growled softly. "I am going to call you Bella. It's Italian for beautiful. Yes, Bella is the only name you will answer to from now on. Bella." I repeated the name one last time before bending and sucking on the tip of that perfect ear, my breath cool. She shivered in response, allowing me to cage her closer. I knew I had her. I went home with her that night. Don't get me wrong! The lady wasn't an easy fuck. We clicked, gelled, talked all night and until recently hadn't spent a night apart.

Meeting her coincided with a quiet period in my employment. The early days as a couple, don't laugh at this but we were together, really together, a committed couple. Anyway, that time had been free from stress. Well, up to a point. I mean, this job and stress do go together. Called out on a regular basis back then held an ease long gone, and my Bella understood what I had to do. My Bella understood many things, trusted me without questioning motives. Her continued faith in me warmed my soul. Not once did she question the fact I had given her the same name held by my charge, my little ward.

I know what you're thinking but no, there's nothing inappropriate here, so get anything like that out of your fucking head. Little Bella is my job, my duty.

Looking after her means protecting her, guarding her against all harm. The name, Bella, is something I like but then I like the Italian language. Watchers learn to speak many languages as part of our training. Italian is my favourite.

Moving on, Bella's faith in my ability to keep my job and my home life separate floored me. I felt honoured with her trust and worked hard to ensure my duties didn't impact on our lives. We were so happy, both of us. *What changed?* I shrugged, an insincere shrug for I knew full well I feared answers. *Never bullshit a bullshitter. Fuck, I knew damn well what had changed.*

I sighed, pushed my frustrations away, and let my hand cup her cheek. We stayed this way for a small precious moment until the chill distracted me. Winter, nastier than normal, a vicious cow of a season, joined the ticking clock to remind me I had to go. Cold touched my toes, wound itself up my calves, my knees and thighs and I couldn't help the shiver, couldn't stop it as the insidious evil jumped torsos. I had to go. There were things that needed doing.

First though, reassurance had to be given. Bella spoke true, a straight to the gut true. Things were worse. A fragile wisp, she needed soft words, not lies, not truth either but words, words I could give her. My Bella had intelligence, both intellectual and emotional and my Bella needed words to give her security, strength. The shivering, mine increased. *Fuck, it was beginning. I had to go.*

"I need you to be whole. Do you understand? Whole."

"Yes, I know. Don't worry."

My hand caressed her cheek, my thumb slid across her bottom lip before I bent and sucked it gently. I let go, placing a kiss on the smooth forehead. "Be my brave girl. I promise to return as quickly as I can. I always do, don't I?"

"I'll wait right here. This is my favourite room. It's where I keep all my treasures and you are the most treasured thing I have. I'll wait for you, always."

The quiet voice, touched with tenderness, and coloured by fear, hurt my heart. I did have one despite how I behaved. My gut, already a volcano of orange, leaped to a fierce red. She nodded, the movement of her head jerky, the angles of light across her cheek bones highlighting her pallor, I felt a piercing sense of panic, flames rising from the pit of my body to my chest and throat. With it came an overwhelming urge to memorise every detail before me, every tiny pore, freckle, and hair in her possession.

My woman had become a jigsaw puzzle. I wondered if the pieces would fit when I returned. Her pieces, my pieces, the jigsaw pieces didn't fit the way they should. The puzzle was harder to solve these days, the pieces not aged; they were worn, tattered. I thought of them like vertebrae. Deterioration clawed fiercely to impinge and destroy, bringing forth a cruel crunching as each piece tried desperately to find comfort. Bone on bone could never be comfortable.

Fuck, it was cold. I don't remember it this cold. See, my Bella had messed my head and even this dark, dingy, narrow hallway I had traversed for fucking forever, today held the power to faze me. How many times had I walked this path without looking back? This time, I looked back. My emotions felt raw, torn. I feared leaving her. Bella deserved better, deserved more. The moment had arrived, the moment to face certain realities clawed at my throat sending bile into a mouth dry with tension.

Further into the long claustrophobic void I felt it, that icy slide that took over my body slowly like a silken garment tantalising me, without the pleasure that is supposed to partner it. I felt it take me over, melt into my skin and possess me. It was like the prep before the procedure, the pre-anaesthetic pill to dull the senses. *Where did I find the courage?* My job had dangers, repercussions I had managed to keep at bay. How much longer could I do that?

I was so tired these days. I wanted to give in, to let it happen, let her die, her, the other one, the woman my Bella feared so passionately. Lately, she brought doubt into all I did, all I saw, not Bella, the other one, Issa. My choices niggled at the edges of my consciousness every time Issa spoke. The power to thrust doubts aside had long left me. I could no more change my profession now than I could stop breathing. *Fuck self-doubt!* I knew my job. I heard the call. I answered. Burning eyes, red-rimmed and with the itch signifying tears I plodded on. I had to. No-one else could do this. The burning increased. The tears did not fall.

I walked and walked and walked some more, and with each step I felt my body tense, fill with the necessary blood I would need. It heated my insides me even as I continued to shiver and shake. *Are you wondering why I hadn't put on warmer clothes?* It doesn't work that way. There are perks to my employment. One of those includes the ability of my body to automatically adjust to the weather but that was under normal circumstances, my life away from the job. Unfortunately, the job itself made other demands in the way of bodily reactions. The more volatile the situation the worse the toll on my body, or our body, those of Watchers in general.

Sometimes it was cold, the kind that makes me feel brittle, breakable, kind of the same way Bella looks. The ice gets into every pore, every single angle, every piece of skin and it dissects your spirit. That cold, that ruthless, insidious, deceptive slide along my bloodstream chilling me from the inside out was the definition of cruel. And yet, I still preferred it to the heat. That bastard sears the souls and burns the spirit to nothing, not even ashes. How was that possible and why was it necessary? How many times had I pondered this same question? Why the fuck was it taking so long to get there this time?

I stumbled, reached backwards to lean against the wall. Something was wrong. Slumping, I gave in to my body's desire to soften, go limp, and slid down the wall until I found myself sitting cross-legged, breathing deeply, my head in my hands. My sadly battered brain fought a losing battle against the memories roaming in a kaleidoscope of colour, tormentingly graphic. They flashed like a power point presentation: that first briefing, going before the forum, the first encounter with the child, meeting my Bella, and the nightmare moments of in-between those days and the now. Why is it we remember the bad part so clearly? Not to say I don't remember the good, but those bad moments have talons and they cut deep.

<u>Emotions in Eruption</u> (now available as an eBook and a paperback)

This part of my writing is so different to the novels. I stumbled into poetry and I love it and somehow it took over and created its own life and place in my work. I thought, why not?

From **Cherry Blossoms** (My love affair with Japan)

Cherry pink blossom

Blood on white petals

joyous harmony

From **Reflections**

On Thinking Too Much

How to make it stop

so that it recedes, disappears,

this constant turning of thoughts

that haunt me even in

those precious moments

when joy, exists?

I did not want to feel

I was right. But, the

need to take a chance

was stronger than

I expected and so I entered

that frightening world.

No peace there because

I was right.

And now pain pierces painfully.

I am scarred, bruised and

lonely when before I was

just alone.

I was wrong to believe in

fairy tales, and white horses, and

handsome heroes.

Now with cold certainty

I must learn to forget

how to read.

From **Reality**

Competition

In the market place of

sheer commodity

you wonder fiercely

about your oddity.

Exclusivity is your sole aim.

But, the playing board denotes

a violent game.

Questions fly with deadly speed.

Voracity must rise to meet the need.

So, you cry choose me, choose me

and have no patience

then to wait and see and

life revolves around the passion

that kills, destroys and

mutilates compassion.

You need to stay alert to read the news.

You must be on top to get the clues.

Those paradigms are flying fast

and you need to be the first not last.

Open eyes and listen well.

Prepare to run upon the bell.

From **Next**

Seasons in Turmoil

What happened to Spring?

When did the Summer go?

What was I doing

to miss the arrival?

How did I not know?

Autumn,

the best of all.

Autumn,

varied, full of sweet reflections,

and bitter moments and yet

Autumn,

the best of all, magic because

aging, when the process is styled,

has dignity, and the slide from

gold to brown is

a caressing, warming chill

heralding acceptance and

becomes a mentor to all

the things to come and

the mentor becomes a

friend to all the things left behind.

Every day reaches out

to the brightest stars and their soft,

shining, sprinkled delicate dust adds

a hopeful flavour to the menu the

Universe is still serving.

I am not impatient for the Winter.

I wait for knowing I will find

the comfort of blankets.

Why not?

I bought them a long time ago.

Thank you for reading this far

Barbara Strickland

www.ingramcontent.com/pod-product-compliance
Lightning Source LLC
Chambersburg PA
CBHW030642110726
47901CB00002B/536